My

Stephen Poliakoff, born in December 1952, was appointed writer in residence at the National Theatre for 1976, and the same year he won the *Evening Standard*'s Most Promising Playwright Award for *Hitting Town* and *City Sugar*.

His plays and films include *Clever Soldiers* (1974), *The Carnation Gang* (1974), *Hitting Town* (1975), *City Sugar* (1975), *Heroes* (1975), *Strawberry Fields* (1977), *Stronger than the Sun* (1977), *Shout Across the River* (1978), *American Days* (1979), *The Summer Party* (1980), *Bloody Kids* (1980), *Caught on a Train* (winner of the BAFTA Award for Best Single Play 1980), *Favourite Nights* (1981), *Soft Targets* (1982), *Runners* (1983), *Breaking the Silence* (1984), *Coming in to Land* (1987), *Hidden City* (1988), *She's Been Away* (winner of five awards at the Venice Film Festival 1989), *Playing with Trains* (1989), *Close My Eyes* (winner of the *Evening Standard*'s Best British Film Award 1991), *Sienna Red* (1992), *Century* (1994), *Sweet Panic* (1996), *Blinded by the Sun* (winner of the Critics' Circle Best Play Award 1996), *The Tribe* (1997), *Food of Love* (1998), *Talk of the City* (1998) and *Remember This* (1999).

Shooting the Past (1999) won the Prix Italia and the Royal Television Society Drama Serial Award, and *Perfect Strangers* (2001) won the Dennis Potter Award (The Writer's Award) at the BAFTAs and the Royal Television Society Awards for Serials & Single Drama and Writer in 2002. *The Lost Prince* (2003) was winner of three Emmy Awards in 2005 including Outstanding Mini Series, followed by *Friends and Crocodiles* (2006) and *Gideon's Daughter* (2006) which won two Golden Globes and a Peabody Award in 2007. His most recent work for the BBC includes *Joe's Palace*, *Capturing Mary* and *A Real Summer* (all 2007), and his latest feature film, *Glorious 39*, was released in 2009.

Stephen Poliakoff

My City

Methuen Drama

Published by Methuen Drama 2011

Methuen Drama, an imprint of Bloomsbury Publishing Plc

1 3 5 7 9 10 8 6 4 2

Methuen Drama
Bloomsbury Publishing Plc
49–51 Bedford Square
London WC1B 3DP
www.methuendrama.com

First published by Methuen Drama in 2011

ISBN: 978 1 408 15963 7

A CIP catalogue record for this book is available from the British Library

Available in the USA from Bloomsbury Academic & Professional, 175 Fifth
Avenue/3rd Floor, New York, NY 10010. www.BloomsburyAcademicUSA.com.

Typeset by Mark Heslington Ltd, Scarborough, North Yorkshire
Printed and bound in Great Britain by CPI Group (UK) Ltd, Croydon CR0 4YY

My City

My City premiered at the Almeida Theatre, London on 8 September 2011, and featured the following cast:

Richard	Tom Riley
Lambert	Tracey Ullman
Minken	David Troughton
Summers	Sorcha Cusack
Julie	Siân Brooke
Waitress	Hannah Arterton

Writer and director Stephen Poliakoff
Design and costume design Lez Brotherston
Lighting Oliver Fenwick
Sound and music Ben and Max Ringham

Characters

Lambert
Richard
Minken
Summers
Julie
Waitress

The time is the present.

Act One

Scene One

The stage is splashed with evening light. It is initially empty except for a bench and an environmentally styled litter bin, suggesting an urban space, a small park. On the back wall a large stone face is staring out, an ornamental feature with flowing locks and penetrating eyes. A piece of urban decoration, the face has a nautical feel, like a sea god emerging.

On the bench a middle-aged woman is lying fully stretched out, her head turned away from us. She is wearing a very elegant coat. City bells are ringing out, pouring across the stage, making a celebratory sound.

Richard *enters, dressed in a summer suit and talking into his mobile. He is in his late twenties or early thirties, and has an intelligent face and a charming fluent manner. He is aware of the figure on the bench, but for a moment doesn't focus on her. As he talks into the phone, his tone is intimate.*

Richard   No, I thought I might drop by . . . because I want to see you of course. No, I just thought it might be nice to do it tonight . . . why? (*Softly.*) Because I haven't seen you for a while . . . no I'm not far away . . . I'm by the river, just been to a party across from St Paul's. Can you hear the bells?

The figure on the bench stirs. **Richard** *glances over for a longer look, then back into the phone.*

Sorry . . . (*Soft, intimate.*) There is a slight distraction here . . . something's going on . . . No . . . I won't stay for long . . .

The figure moves again, making a murmuring sound.

I'll phone you back, in a moment. Just got to investigate something.

He rings off. The figure half turns her head.

Richard *watching her.*

Excuse me . . .

The figure sits up slowly, a fine-looking woman, beautifully dressed.
Richard *moves a pace towards her.*

Forgive me staring, I just wondered if you were alright?

The figure looks up at **Richard**, *very poised and untroubled.*

You obviously are . . .

Lambert   I am, yes.

Richard *is suddenly riveted.*

Richard   This is terribly rude, I don't mean to stare, this
is extraordinary, for me anyway . . . Miss Lambert, it is you
isn't it?!

Lambert   Yes.

Richard   This is amazing! (*He smiles.*) I suddenly saw it was
you . . . (*He stares across at her again.*) I'm sorry. It is such a
surprise! You won't remember me . . . Richard Kenton.

Lambert *looks at him, studying him.*

Lambert   Richard Kenton . . .

Richard   Yes, you taught me, years and years ago at
primary school. Your school! You won't remember of course.

Lambert   Richard Kenton? (*Momentary pause.*) Yes, I
remember you.

Richard   You do?

Lambert   Absolutely.

Richard   That's incredible . . . but I was tiny! I was this size
. . . (*He indicates a figure about three feet high.*) Or maybe not
quite that size, since I was fourteen the very last time I saw
you. I came back to school for a visit . . . so probably a little
bigger – (*He holds his hand a little higher.*) Maybe about here
. . . You look just the same.

Lambert   Thank you Richard. Although I'm sure that's not true.

Richard   You look terrific, younger even.

Lambert   Well that *certainly* can't be true.

Richard   It's such a coincidence . . . I came out for some fresh air, to make a phone call, and suddenly you were there.

He stops and looks across at her on the bench.

Lambert *meets his look.*

Lambert   I was just having a pause.

Richard   A pause?

Lambert   Yes, I was having an evening stroll, I decided to take a pause . . . on this bench.

Richard   Of course, how perfectly natural.

Lambert (*chuckles*)   Is it? I don't make a habit of lying stretched out on benches in the open air. But today I was.

Richard   And I woke you up.

Lambert   Oh I wasn't asleep.

Richard (*smiles*)   Right . . . I can't believe you remember me!

Lambert   But I do.

Richard   How is that possible? All those thousands of kids that have been through that school . . . little podgy faces with their teeth missing, they must look so alike. You can't remember them all surely?

Lambert   Certainly not, no. Most are a blur naturally . . . (*looking across at* **Richard**) but a few stand out.

Richard   I don't think I'll ask why – could be a dangerous question!

Lambert   I remember you, but I'm not saying I would have recognised you. You look very smart Richard.

Richard   I'm not normally in a suit as it happens – but I've been at the summer party where I work . . . it's just back there. And it seems rather perfect anyway, for our meeting I mean. As do those bells! (**Lambert** *looks at him.*) You were always making us listen to what was going on, the sounds outside the window of the classroom. (*He smiles.*)

Lambert (*opening her handbag and beginning to look for something*)   Is that so?

Richard (*glancing upstage*)   I'm not so sure about that face though – a piece of rather odd decoration isn't it! Who do you think it is? Neptune?

Lambert (*still peering into her bag*)   I usually have a little chocolate around this time. I have half a bar I'd saved somewhere in here . . . I think you'll find it is Titus Meredith.

Richard   Titus Meredith? Of course! (*Momentary pause. He smiles.*) I'm sure I've heard of him, I just need the smallest of clues –

Lambert   Ah there it is. (*She produces a piece of chocolate in silver foil.*) Not many people have heard of Titus Meredith.

Richard   Good. What did he do to earn his place on that wall then?

Lambert   He was an actor who got himself murdered.

She shuts her bag with a firm click.

He was taking a walk in the pleasure gardens that used to run along the river here and he was killed on this exact spot.

She breaks off a small piece of chocolate and eats it.

Richard   He was murdered right here?

Lambert   Yes. Where that face is now. His throat was cut.

Richard   Why?

Lambert   The murder was never solved. It started the other side of the river with a furious argument outside the stage door of the old Drury Lane Theatre, swords were drawn, a barrow of apples was knocked over –

Richard   You know the details too!

Lambert   The apples are important. Somebody followed Titus across the river and murdered him in the gardens as people were strolling past and the band played. His ghost occasionally pops up it is said around here, *and* in the stalls of the Theatre Royal Drury Lane.

Richard   A ghost that haunts two places?

Lambert   That's right. A busy ghost. There's a faint rustle and then the sound of somebody biting sharply into a fresh apple.

Richard   Great, the sound of an apple being bitten into becoming terrifying . . . (*He turns.*) And now they've made a suitably creepy garden out of it.

Lambert   That's right.

Richard   I knew you'd know who it was. You always knew!

Lambert   Well that isn't true Richard.

Now I must get on, it was a very pleasant surprise to run into you. (*She smiles.*) It always is, to meet old children.

Richard   You're going to go now?

Lambert   Yes. I have to.

Richard   I can't tempt you into a pub for a quick drink (*he smiles*), and a bag of salt and vinegar crisps?

Lambert   Not today, no.

Richard   But another time?

Lambert (*moving*)   Maybe.

Richard   I could arrange for Julie to be there.

Lambert   Julie?

Richard   Julie Shannon, you probably don't remember but you used to keep us behind together after class. I'm still in touch with her as it happens. She would be thrilled to see you I know. (**Lambert** *turns.*) She loved your stories.

Lambert   We'll see. I'm a little busy at the moment.

She moves again.

Richard   Can I take your number?

Lambert *stops.*

Lambert   You can give me your number.

Richard   Great, I'll give you my mobile number. Shall I put it in your phone?

Lambert   I don't have a mobile phone.

Richard   You don't?!

Lambert (*lightly*)   I'm one of only eight people in the whole city apparently who doesn't have a mobile phone. Just say it to me, your number, and I'll remember it.

Richard   Just say it?

Lambert   Yes.

Richard   07790 628 940.

Lambert (*without pausing*)   Right.

She begins to move off.

Richard   You've got it?!

Lambert   Yes, I've got it Richard. I'll call you.

Richard (*suddenly*)   What is it?

Lambert *stops.*

Richard   I don't meant to test you or anything . . . I'm sure you've got an amazing memory, but getting it just like that!

Lambert   Seems rather improbable?

Richard   Maybe yes. I just don't want to lose touch, us having bumped into each other.

Momentary pause.

Lambert   07790 628 940. You see I have got it.

Richard   That's brilliant . . . and a little spooky! (*Grins.*) Sorry I shouldn't have said that.

Lambert   It's fine.

She's moving to exit.

Richard   And the number will stay there will it?

Lambert   It will.

Richard   So have you got loads of numbers in your head?

Lambert   I have certain numbers in my head, yes. I *will* ring you Richard.

She turns at exit.

It's really very good to see you looking so well and successful.

She exits. **Richard** *stares after her for a moment. He takes out his phone and dials. We hear two rings and then a female voice.*

Julie (VO)   This is Julie's phone. If you are going to leave a message, make it short.

Richard   Right, it's Richard here, out of the blue as usual! We've not talked for ages I know. Anyway how is this for short – I just met Miss Lambert, she was lying on a bench in the open air, picture that Julie! She talked of ghosts.

Do you want to see her? . . . Is that short enough?

He rings off.

Blackout.

FIRST ASSEMBLY

The sound of heavy rain and children's voices singing a hymn to a piano accompaniment. As the bench and the litter bin are removed **Minken** *walks on stage. A man of similar age to* **Lambert***, he is dressed in a dark suit and a pale tie. He has a very precise manner. He is carrying a large clock face that he hangs over the face of Titus Meredith on the back wall. It shows it is 9 o'clock.*

The singing is rising to a crescendo. **Minken** *is joined on stage by* **Summers***, a thin faced woman of the same age. She is dressed all in black. As the singing reaches its last bars,* **Lambert** *walks on stage in a summer dress, her manner more youthful than in the previous scene. Her tone is authoritative but warm.* **Minken** *and* **Summers** *stand on either side of her, but a few paces back, staring out impassively. Next to each of them is a small desk with a large box on it.*

The children stop singing and fall silent. There is an expectant rustle.

Lambert   For some of you this is your first day – and first days in a new place can be very frightening I know, especially on a dark rainy day like today. Everything can look alarming, including me. And very big. But there will come a time when all this will seem normal – just like it is for those older children right at the back today – and you may be tempted to giggle and talk all the way through, and of course fidget. But I like to think I *will* always be able to stop you fidgeting. We will see.

We meet every morning here to tell stories and imagine things. And usually, nearly always, Mr Minken and Miss Summers will be helping me tell the stories, and sometimes you will come up here and tell them yourself.

And quite often we will start just by listening to what is happening outside. Like now, what can we hear? It's raining yes, but through the rain there are other sounds aren't there.

We hear them welling up around us.

The rumble of the city. Your city . . . which we will explore in many ways.

Today I'm going to take you back into the past, a little time-travelling.

The light is changing imperceptibly. **Summers** *moves the hands back on the large clock.*

Lambert   When I was small and people first started trying to teach me, the past, Queen Victoria, Henry VIII, the Romans, all seemed to be happening at the same time. Long ago was one place jumbled up together, and nobody really tried to straighten it out for me, not for a long time.

So I'm going to try it this way, just with this building and the room we're sitting in.

What if we went back to when your parents were small, what would they have heard outside that window? If they had been sitting cross-legged on this floor?

Minken *and* **Summers** *sit at the small tables. They remove the boxes. On each table is a manual typewriter.*

They start typing furiously.

Lambert   This is the sound they would have heard from the school office, and then from outside the window would have come more typing from the offices in the building across the playground wall. On a summer's day, when all the windows were open . . .

Minken *and* **Summers** *still typing vigorously, but all around us we hear the sound of typing.*

Lambert   There would have been a symphony of typing, and clanking as well because every now and then you would have heard the copying machine, the old Gestetner machine thumping into life, with its purple ink . . . (*We hear the* *clanking of a Gestetner.*) because that's how they made copies of things in those days.

The sound of the typewriters and the copying machine reach a crescendo and then cut out suddenly.

And if we go back, past your grandparents' time to your great grandparents' time, when that building across the playground was a piano warehouse, and there was the sound of thirty pianos stopping and starting, being tried out.

Minken *and* **Summers** *still typing, but the sound changes to that of many pianos.*

Lambert   And now if we go back further . . . a big jump here, another hundred years, when stagecoaches pulled by four horses would have come really close.

The sound of pianos turns into the sound of many spinets, an echoing ghostly music mingling with the sound of a stagecoach.

This part of north London was a small village and when it rained as hard as it is now, mud poured along the street like a river. Somebody who was here then was the famous American writer Edgar Allan Poe. He was a pupil at a school that stood on the very same spot as this room . . . he said this was a misty-looking village where there was a vast number of gigantic and gnarled trees. So outside that window, there would have been a line of tremendous terrifying trees –

There is an extremely loud clap of thunder.

I didn't plan that children! (*She smiles.*) That was a real clap of thunder, it wasn't on Mr Minken's tapes, where the other sounds come from . . .

Minken (*standing up*)   It was a lucky accident. The thunder is directly above us.

But there is no need to be afraid. No need at all.

Another clap of thunder.

Lambert (*warm smile*)   You are safe here. Quite safe. On another day Mr Minken will tell you why thunder happens, but for now we'll stay in the time of the mud and the giant trees.

Minken *takes his jacket off.*

Lambert   And we're going to travel together into a yard, which was where our playground wall is now. One day the man who wrote the hymn you just sang, John Wesley, walked past that yard and he saw one of the most extraordinary things he had ever seen. In the yard was an enormous Newfoundland dog – you have to imagine Mr Minken as a very large dog.

Minken   When I take my jacket off you know that is the time to imagine me into a different shape – today it is a huge dog.

Lambert   And also in the yard was a raven – you have to imagine Miss Summers as a large black bird with a shiny beak.

Summers *sitting all in black turns her head sharply.*

Lambert   And the bird and the dog had fallen deeply in love, they could not bear to be apart. And the raven, for they are very good mimics, had learnt to bark exactly like the dog. And when the dog went out for a walk, the raven howled with sadness, and she would collect sticks and scraps and little bones as presents ready for his return.

Here children is an amazing love story, a bird in love with a gigantic dog.

We hear a dog barking and an answering high-pitched bark.

Minken   That happened just through that very window there, right next to our school wall.

Lambert   It sounds like a fairy story – but it is true. So when you run out into the playground at break time, stop for a moment and imagine you can hear the dog and the raven barking at each other from all those years ago.

Blackout.

We hear the sound of a stagecoach roaring towards us, turning into a burst of Vivaldi, as the clock face and the two tables and typewriters are taken off. The face of Titus Meredith is no longer on the back wall; instead a large fan-shaped vent is visible, dark and urban, like might be found in a shopping mall.

Scene Two

The Vivaldi burst changes into The Four Seasons *arranged as piped music seeping through the speakers. The back wall glows a shiny antiseptic colour around the fan-shaped vent. There are black cafe chairs and three white tables. The name of the cafe, The Zanzibar, is projected down the side of the back wall, the letters arranged at an angle and decreasing in size.*

Julie *is sitting at one of the tables. She is the same age as* **Richard**, *and is strikingly dressed in an individual, slightly bohemian style, stylish rather than eccentric. She has a north London accent and a vibrant direct manner.*

The **Waitress**, *a young woman in her twenties, is wiping one of the tables.*

Julie   I hope you don't mind me asking, but you can't do anything about the music can you?

Waitress (*blankly*)   The music?

Julie   I use the term loosely of course, but you couldn't switch it off for a moment?

Waitress   I can't no. We're not allowed to touch it. It's on a timer.

Julie   A timer, really? And how does that work, timed to what? Does it ever stop?

Waitress   It does stop sometimes. Not very often. But then it starts again.

Julie   Right . . . well let's hope we're lucky then.

Waitress   Can I get you anything?

Julie   Yeah, when my friend comes. That's OK, isn't it, me sitting here till then? It's not as if it's very busy.

Waitress   No, no, the whole mall's been a bit empty since it opened. Not many people reach us up here on the highest level anyway, especially in the evenings like now. We've got more levels than any other shopping mall in London.

Julie (*smiles*)   Don't expect many people know that.

Waitress   No, I spend a lot of time by those railings, staring down at the tiny dots.

Julie   And that's an interesting sign you have there . . . (*She squints across at it.*) The Zanzibar . . . but arranged like an eye test!

Richard *enters*.

Julie   At last there you are!

Richard (*his tone familiar*)   At last?! What do you mean? She's not here yet, so what's the problem?

Julie   We were going to have a little time to prepare remember.

Richard   And we have. There is absolutely no need to be nervous.

Julie   And I'm not. (*Immediately to* **Waitress**.) I'll have a triple espresso please, and he'll have a cappuccino with an extra sprinkling of chocolate on top, and a Danish, the kind with an apricot in the middle. (*Turns to* **Richard**.) That's right isn't it?

Richard   Absolutely.

Julie   Well it doesn't vary does it!

Waitress   That's a *triple* espresso is it?

Julie   Yeah, that's definitely what I need.

The **Waitress** *exits.*

The music is non-negotiable apparently. I hope she doesn't mind piped Vivaldi –

Richard   No, she chose this spot after all. (*He looks at her.*) Nice clothes Julie!

Julie   Well I thought because it's her – and after all this time – I should make a real effort. (*Familiar tone.*) And are you good Richard?

Richard (*breezily*)   I am, yes, at the moment, very good. Things are full of promise. It's a year and four months since I last saw you.

Julie   That's about our average isn't it? I didn't realise you kept count quite like that.

Richard   Yeah, I like keeping track of time. I thought about you three weeks ago for some reason on a bus.

Julie   I last thought about you at the dentist, just as I was gripping the side of the chair. (*Suddenly.*) So we're here because you found her on a bench?

Richard   That's right.

Julie   What was she doing on the bench?

Richard   I don't know.

Julie   You didn't ask?

Richard   No, believe it or not I didn't, not directly. It's not the easiest question. She said she was having a pause.

Julie   *I* would have found out. (*She moves.*) Aren't you a little scared? Just a fraction?

Richard   Scared? Julie for Christ sake, what is there to be scared about?

Lambert *enters.*

Richard   Miss Lambert!

Lambert *is dressed in a beautiful light coat over an elegant summer dress.*

Lambert   Hello Richard. (*She looks across at* **Julie**.)

Julie   Julie, Julie Shannon. (*She moves forward to shake hands. She can't tell if* **Lambert** *remembers her or not.*)

Lambert   Of course it's Julie, yes, how lovely to see you.

Julie   Thanks. I won't count the number of years it's been.

Lambert   No.

Julie   Richard knows of course, down to the exact date probably.

Richard   Yes.

Momentary pause.

Julie   You look tremendous.

Richard   Even more than last time.

Lambert   Thank you.

The **Waitress** *enters with the coffees, the Danish and a third drink in a glass.*

Waitress   Triple espresso, cappuccino with Danish, and one vodka.

Richard   We didn't order a vodka.

Lambert   That's for me.

Julie (*to* **Waitress**)   You knew she was coming? How did you know her order? (*Nervous laugh.*) That's weird.

Lambert   I'm usually here at this time, and Clare knows what I want to drink.

Waitress   I saw her join you, and I knew she'd want her regular. (*To* **Lambert**.) Is everything alright? Want anything else?

Lambert   That's perfect Clare.

The **Waitress** *exits.*

Julie   And the music's stopped! Have they switched it off for you?

Richard   That's very impressive.

Lambert   Yes, well we can't have piped Vivaldi can we, (*she smiles*) might spoil our meeting.

Julie   You go on shopping binges here do you?

Lambert   No Julie, but this place is new, and I like to keep in touch, see how the city's changing. (*She picks up the glass.*) Cheers!

Julie   Cheers! If you can, with a triple espresso.

Lambert *knocks back the vodka in one hit.*

Lambert   So you two have remained in touch all this time?

Richard   Well it's very much our own version of keeping in touch – which means I phone Julie about every three months and she never *ever* phones me back! And then suddenly she'll pop up a few months later, early in the morning, her voice rasping out –

Julie   Not rasping, I don't rasp –

Richard   Or I'll get a sudden text, 'How the fuck are you? What the fuck are you up to?' (*Suddenly realises.*) I, I'm so sorry Miss Lambert.

Julie   He's a little nervous. Yeah, so we keep in contact. He likes to talk and I like to text.

Lambert   That's unusual because you were so young . . .
amongst girls maybe, but you two, a lifelong friendship –
that's a rare thing.

Richard   Well there's an obvious reason for that isn't there.

Lambert   Is there?

Julie   There is absolutely no reason why you should
remember it of course, but perhaps you do. Richard and me,
we had a problem.

Richard   A difficulty, rather than a problem.

Pause.

Lambert   I saw a great many kids over the years –

Richard   Millions of kids, naturally! You can't remember
the micro detail of their lives, how could you? (*To* **Julie**.) She
won't remember exactly how we were.

Julie (*she turns*)   I was incredibly dyslexic Miss Lambert, I
couldn't read at all, even big notices in the street – I couldn't
make sense of them.

Richard   And I couldn't concentrate and I couldn't spell.

Julie   Neither of us could spell . . . not remotely!

Richard   It was like my brain was overloading, bursting
with things, it went on these sort of riffs of its own which I
couldn't stop, attention deficit disorder, but maybe worse! I
couldn't sit still, I couldn't listen, I couldn't be on time.

Julie   I couldn't even spell cheese . . . or bucket!

Richard   When I spoke I could sound very fluent for a
while, then suddenly it would short circuit and I would have
this terrible stammer.

Julie   And for me trying to read a book was torture! And
I took everything literally, figures of speech drove me mad
– 'don't look like that, the wind might change', I thought
about that for months for instance . . .

Richard   And because we were the worst in the school, we were drawn to each other.

Julie   A connection –

Richard   We often knew what the other was thinking.

Julie   Well Richard knew what *I* was thinking – because he is a lot better at that than me . . . And you encouraged us to be together a lot, and you spent time alone with us, because our parents weren't interested –

Richard   – had no patience with us. And your stories –

Julie   Of course your stories . . .! A lot of things began to make sense after them.

Richard   They were the only things I could sit and listen to.

Julie   And so we got better. I began to read – (*sharp grin, indicating the sign*) I can even read the name of this place, and he stammered less.

Richard   So me running into you the other day, allows us to say thank you.

Julie   For helping us. Because it was a real nightmare not being able to decode things and now we can. (*She smiles.*) Most of the time!

Richard (*indicating* **Julie**)   And that's why we've kept in touch.

Julie (*to* **Lambert**)   Of course you can't remember any of this I realise . . . how we were.

Pause.

Lambert   I was going to say – I've seen many kids over the years obviously, but I remember Julie and Richard and their difficulties very well.

Julie (*startled*)   You do?

Richard   We clearly were the worst then!

Lambert   You were particularly distinctive shall we say.

Julie   Well you did a bloody good job.

Richard   You did.

Lambert   That's very kind. I appreciate it.

Silence. They look at her.

Julie (*firmly*)   So . . .

Lambert   So?

Julie   So now we've done that, I can ask what on earth were you doing lying on a bench when Richard found you?

Slight pause.

Lambert   On a bench? Was I?

Julie (*flashing out of her*)   If you can remember us when we were tiny, you definitely know what you were doing when Richard found you the other day!

Lambert (*calmly*)   Of course I remember. I just don't see what's odd about it.

Julie   Why were you like that?

Lambert   I was having a pause.

Richard   I told you that's what she was doing.

Julie   A pause from what?

Silence for a moment.

Lambert   I go for walks at night. (*Looks straight at both of them.*) Most nights.

Richard   Most nights?!

Julie   Don't you sleep? Is it you can't sleep?

Lambert   I find some interesting times to sleep, different parts of the day.

Julie   You never sleep during the night?

Lambert   No, not really no.

Richard   You've become completely nocturnal then?

Lambert   Yes. The walks are very invigorating across the city at night. Not many people are around. I have two or three launching-off spots where I start to walk, this shopping mall is one of them.

Julie   You walk alone?

Lambert   Yes.

Julie   Is that safe?

Lambert   Mostly. (*Poised, smile.*) I'm hardly going to be mistaken for a lady of the night.

Richard   Let's get this straight, you criss-cross the city night after night, entirely on your own?

Lambert   Yes.

Richard   Walking and walking?

Lambert   And sitting.

Richard   In districts you don't know, you've never been to before?

Lambert   Frequently, yes.

Silence. They both look at her.

Richard   Why do you walk at night Miss Lambert?

Lambert   Why do I do it?

Momentary pause.

The only reason I can give you is because I like it. It's what I want to do with my nights.

Richard   That's the only reason!

Julie   Is it because the teaching's finished? You're no longer a head teacher?

Lambert   No, it started before I left, the night walking.

Julie   Was it something personal? A big relationship ended?

Lambert (*lightly*)   A big relationship? That certainly isn't the reason, no.

Richard (*suddenly*)   Did something weird happen in the school perhaps? Something dodgy?

Lambert   Something dodgy? What could you have in mind Richard?

Julie   A scandal of some sort?

Lambert   A scandal? You mean like Mrs Hoolerman?

Richard   Mrs Hoolerman! What a fantastic name, who is she?

Lambert   She was head of the school on the Green, the only other school in the area, apart from mine, that had great results.

Richard   Two model schools . . .

Lambert   She was a very beautiful proud woman. A tremendous head by all accounts, and a wonderful teacher.

Julie   What happened to Mrs Hoolerman?

Lambert   It was very strange what happened to her.

She opens her bag, starting to look for something.

Julie   You can't stop now!

Richard   Go on, you have to tell us the story Miss Lambert.

Lambert   It's not a story.

Lambert *closes her bag with a sharp click, without taking out what she was looking for.*

Lambert   I got a message from Mrs Hoolerman, 'You must come and see me immediately Elizabeth, and I mean immediately, within the hour.'

Well I couldn't do that, but I went to see her that same day. She is standing by the window in her office. She was always beautifully dressed, but invariably in dark colours, and today she is all in black –

Richard   Somebody's dead?

Lambert   She looks straight at me and says, 'You and I have always done everything for our schools haven't we Elizabeth?'

I see no reason to disagree with this, so I reply, 'Yes we have Rachel.'

Her lip starts to quiver, 'So you will find what I'm about to tell you truly shocking. They say I have misappropriated school funds and that I have been doing so on a regular basis for many years. Isn't that *incredible*?!'

I do find it incredible, I ask, 'What exactly are they saying you did?'

'Well one of the more absurd things they say I did was that I took funds from my school – my *own* school – to pay for a new carpet in my home, a new sofa and forty-four-inch TV! – And even more ludicrous than that, they say I went to stay at the Ritz hotel in Paris and charged it as a school trip! Me, Rachel Hoolerman, responsible for some of the best results for eleven-year-olds in the country! It's a plot of course . . . '

'A plot by whom?' I ask.

'By a sinister group within the governors and the local authority who have been plotting my downfall for years. They refuse to accept my word – that I did go to Paris but it was with someone of national importance who paid for everything and who's identity cannot be divulged.'

'But the other charges, you can disprove those surely?' I say.

'You don't understand!' she shouts at me. 'There are such forces at work Elizabeth . . . they will come after you next.

It is of course totally out of the question that I have misappropriated a single pound of school funds and you have to tell me right now – you find it impossible, completely *unthinkable*.' And she yells at me, 'GO ON SAY IT!'

And she seems to be shrinking before my eyes, like the witch in *The Wizard of Oz*, shrinking into the floor crying out, 'there are dark forces out there Elizabeth stronger than you and I!'

And that was the end of Rachel Hoolerman. It turned out she had embezzled over three hundred thousand pounds.

Momentary pause.

Julie   Jesus . . .

Richard   Great story . . . the end of Mrs Hoolerman. She felt she was entitled having worked so hard, that she deserved the money!

Lambert (*calmly*)   So no, there was no scandal at my school. None.

She returns to hunting in her bag.

Right,   I was looking for my purse – which I have now found – so I can pay for our drinks.

Richard   Absolutely not. I'm paying for this. (**Lambert** *looks up*.) No argument.

Lambert   That's very kind. But you're only paying for *these* drinks. (*She shuts her bag with a sharp click*.) Not for anything that happens afterwards. And I have a suggestion. I am meeting Mr Minken and Miss Summers a little bit later, would you like to join us?

Richard (*startled*)   You're meeting them *tonight*?

Julie   You're not meeting them here are you?

Lambert   I'm meeting them tonight, yes, but not here exactly, nine levels down.

Julie   Nine levels down? That sounds dangerous!

Lambert (*nonchalantly*)   Yes, the deepest level, the most subterranean you can get here, level zero four. At a bar called Sunquest.

Richard   One's old teachers coming out at night, that's brilliant, how can we resist?

Julie   Difficult to say no I agree. See what they look like now!

Lambert   So you'll come?

Julie   Oh yes.

Richard   Most certainly.

Lambert   Excellent. The Sunquest, go straight past the bar, and into the second room in exactly an hour's time.

Julie   Right . . .

The piped music seeps around them again.

And the music's started again! (*She laughs.*) They must know you're about to make a move Miss Lambert . . . (**Julie** *picks up her bag.*) I need to phone my partner, he is away at the moment, I'm joining him tomorrow. So I'll do that and then I'll do some shopping, what better opportunity! Then I'll meet you all the way down on level zero four.

Lambert   At 8 o'clock.

Julie   At 8 o'clock on the dot. (*She moves off.*) Can't wait . . .

She exits. The piped Vivaldi rises. **Richard** *stares across at* **Lambert**.

Richard   Amazing!

Lambert   What's amazing?

Richard   Seeing you. And I'm about to see them. (*Relaxed smile.*) It's exciting.

Lambert   That's good.

Richard   And I'll be able to watch you set off for tonight's walk perhaps? Maybe even get to accompany you?

Lambert (*lightly*)   That certainly won't happen, no.

The **Waitress** *enters with the bill and pin machine.*

Richard   The bill arrives without us even asking for it!

Lambert   That's because she knows I never stay long.

Waitress   That's right she never does.

Lambert (*handing the* **Waitress** *her glass*)   Thank you Clare, see you tomorrow.

(*To* **Richard**.) And I will see you down in the basement.

Richard   Level zero four . . . yes. (**Lambert** *moves to exit.*) I'll stay here, and eat my Danish, (*he smiles*) very slowly.

Lambert *exits.* **Richard** *stares after her for a moment.*

Richard   I wonder what she has gone off to do . . . (*He turns to the waitress and pin machine.*) I think I'll pay by cash if you don't mind . . . calculating tips on these machines, pushing the right buttons, it can cause me problems, even now! I end up screaming at them.

Waitress   We don't want that, no.

Richard   She used to teach me you know, Miss Lambert, when I was little.

Waitress   Right . . .

Richard   Does she come here every day . . . ?

Waitress   Three times a week. And always at the same time. And always the same drink.

Richard   And always alone?

Waitress   Yes.

Richard (*looking for change in his jacket pocket*)   You're
thinking why is this guy so interested in his ex-primary-
school teacher – (*He smiles at her.*) Sorry I shouldn't tell you
what you are thinking . . .

Waitress   No . . . but I *was* thinking that, a little.

Richard   Yes . . . (*Momentary pause, his tone relaxed.*) Well if I
riff about school for a second –

'I am sorry I'm so late Miss . . . again!'

'Why are you wearing Thomas's shoes Richard?!' . . .

Never being able to find what I wanted . . . always only
hearing half of anything . . . only sometimes seeing half of
people's faces, everything in double time . . . and then her
stillness in front of me, suddenly slowed everything – so it
came into focus, made things bearable . . . (*He smiles at the*
Waitress.) That's why I'm little curious about her, having
bumped into her again.

Waitress   Right . . .

Richard   So she sits here, three times a week, waiting for
the night . . . (*He smiles.*) That's great.

Blackout.

*The piped Vivaldi lifts in volume and then suddenly bursts into full
rich orchestral sound.*

SECOND ASSEMBLY

Minken *and* **Summers** *enter. There is a row of tiny plastic red chairs along the back wall. The Vivaldi burst dissolves into the sound of children's voices singing a popular song.* **Minken** *and* **Summers** *sit at either end of the row of tiny chairs. The vent on the back wall closes.*

Lambert *enters wearing a different dress to the previous scene. She stands centre stage.*

The children's singing stops.

Lambert   When you're at school, sitting on the floor staring up at assembly like you are now, it is very hard to imagine I know that the teachers there in front of you were ever young, were ever tiny in fact, that they actually had teachers of their own – who may have frightened them, or appeared extremely funny and strange.

Summers *approaches* **Lambert**, *holding a large glass jar. For a moment she stands in the shadows behind her.*

Lambert   But we did. And there were certain things we found so scary at school, maybe we still dream about them . . .!

Lambert *stands back to allow* **Summers** *to take centre stage. She then sits on one of the tiny chairs at the back.*

Summers (*her manner warm, full of energy*)   I was taught by a group of nuns, and the head teacher was a very small woman, a particularly tiny nun in fact, but with a very vicious tongue. (*Irish accent.*) 'That is the silliest thing I have ever heard Geraldine, you really are one of the most stupid children I have ever met. You will get four pebbles – and they will be big ones.'

What did she mean? Each one of us was given an empty sweet jar like this one at the beginning of term, but we were never given any sweets.

Every time we did anything wrong or made a mistake, a pebble was put in our sweet jar.

She drops some pebbles from her pocket into the empty sweet jar.

And when your jar was half full you were beaten across the hand with a ruler six times. So the sound of pebbles going into a glass jar was a truly horrible sound, one you heard in your nightmares. And when your jar was totally full – oh dread the day that happened – you were given 12 strokes of the ruler and made to stand in the window of the head teacher's study for a whole day so everybody who approached the school could see your shame. (*Irish accent.*) 'One of these days if you're not careful, you will find you've been put in a sweet jar yourself Geraldine, and they will screw down the lid and put you on a shelf in the factory where they bottle wicked children.'

She rattles the pebbles in the sweet jar.

Nobody ever believes that's what happened in my school but it did! All these girls with sweet jars full of pebbles and feeling really afraid.

And that is why to this day I don't much like the sight of big glass jars, and I really hate walking on pebbles on the beach – with every step I take I think I might get punished.

Minken *steps forward.* **Summers** *sits back on one of the tiny chairs.*

Minken   My teacher had a wooden leg. It was at my boarding school, where I was sent away to at the age of seven. And as I lay there in the dark dormitory, you could hear the leg coming down the passage. I can still hear the sound of this leg creaking towards me, even today!

We hear the sinister creaking approaching, getting louder.

He would line all the new boys up and we were each given one drawing pin, and you were holding it between your fingers wondering what is it for?

And suddenly he would boom, 'Come up boy, and stick the pin in my leg.'

He lifts one leg up on a chair.

And you approached him, really shaking with fear, holding your drawing pin, and he would roar at you, he had a huge fleshy face, 'Make sure you've got the right leg boy! If you see it bleeding, you know you got the wrong one!'

He pulls up his trouser leg to reveal a piece of wood, full of drawing pins strapped to his leg.

And even though you could see the wooden leg staring at you, you were trembling, thinking is this some kind of trick? (*He shouts.*) 'What are you waiting for boy?!'

With a shaking hand, he pushes the drawing pin into his leg and then yells out.

Sometimes he would yell with pain like that, as the pin went in! And then he would roar with laughter . . .

He walks with the leg covered in drawing pins.

And he would strut up and down in front of us, with his leg completely covered in drawing pins!

So that's why children, as you may have noticed, sometimes my hand will shake when I'm opening a box of drawing pins. And since the school is absolutely full of drawing pins, I find I think about him nearly every day!

Lambert *takes centre stage.*

Lambert   Now my head teacher, yes just like Mr Minken and Miss Summers, I was tiny once – my head was in fact two people, a husband and wife. The husband was very tall and the wife was very very fat. And they would stand up together on stage every morning, as outside we could hear the steam trains setting off.

And often they would start the assembly by having a ferocious spelling competition between the two of them

to wake us all up. (*She turns to* **Minken** *and spits out.*)
'Spell Khrushchev!' (**Minken** *begins to spell it.*) 'Spell
condescension!' . . . she would scream the words out, it was
quite frightening, hardly giving him time to finish. But far
worse than that, she would say, 'Mr Eric will tell you a story
now.' And Mr Eric would start, he had a wonderful voice.

Minken   Once upon a time there was an enormous house
in a secret valley that only I knew how to find. I discovered
how to get there by complete chance when one day a bird
flew in through my bedroom window.

Lambert   And you were spellbound, you were so happy
– and then as often as not, just as he was about half way
through, his wife would yell, 'That's enough Mr Eric!
Children Mr Eric will finish the story tomorrow.' And
tomorrow would come and we never heard the rest of the
story, that happened a lot. We were aching to hear what
came next, but the story was never finished.

It was a special kind of torture.

For years afterwards I used to worry terribly that films for
instance were going to break down in the middle and be
unable to restart. (*She stares out.*) So here is a promise. That is
never something I will do to you. I will never be like Mr Eric.

Blackout.

A burst of classical music, Mozart. **Lambert** *remains on stage for a
moment watching the scene change.*

Scene Three

*The Mozart melts into some piped music, soft rock leaking around
the subterranean space. Two neon strips spring into life, one blue,
one pink, along the back wall, and the vent opens up fully, like a
dark urban flower. In the floor there is a line of small white lights
stretching right across the stage. Initially they are very pale.*

Julie *and* **Richard** *are sitting on bar stools. There are more stools arranged along the side wall.* **Richard** *has a glass of orange juice.*

Julie   This is just a little strange don't you think?

Richard   Why? I rather like this place, 'Sunquest' – deep underground but searching for the sun. (*Grins.*) I wonder if it ever gets really throbbing down here?

Julie   It might not be very wise us doing this Richard.

Richard   Wise? Why shouldn't it be wise, what harm could it possibly do?

Julie   It may be difficult seeing them again, awkward.

Richard   No, I'm sure they'll be very appreciative we stayed for one drink.

Julie (*getting off her stool*)   I don't expect there's anybody in the world who doesn't worry about being judged by their ex-teachers . . .

Richard   Yes there is, I don't.

Julie   Really?

Richard   No I don't. But oddly hardly a month goes by when I don't think about those assemblies they put on for us as kids, with special sounds and props and things. It was my first ever theatre. (*He turns.*) We owe them a drink!

Julie   Yeah, but what if they've become really eccentric? They must be quite old by now mustn't they?

Richard   Yes, both of them will be pretty frail by now, hobbling a little maybe –

Minken *enters carrying a large suitcase. He is immaculately dressed in a dark suit and red tie. He is slightly stockier, but his manner is no less energised than at the assemblies. Everything he does is very precise.*

He enters fast. **Julie** *spins round.*

Julie   Jesus! Is that really you Mr Minken?

Minken   Hello you two! So there you are!

Richard   Mr Minken . . .!

Minken   I hope I'm not late. Am I late?

Julie   No, no we got here early. (*She stretches out her hand and* **Minken** *shakes it formally.*) It's been such a long time.

Minken   Of course, many many years. And you both look just as I imagined you would.

Richard (*sharp smile*)   We're just as you imagined? Maybe that's a little disappointing –

Julie   You look so much younger than I was expecting . . .

Minken   Thank you. A little stouter probably than when we last saw each other, but I try to keep myself in trim. (*Moving his bulky suitcase.*) I'll just put this out of the way.

Richard   Are you going on holiday Mr Minken?

Minken   No, no, I've been collecting a few things from my brother's flat. Some family heirlooms. (*Positioning the suitcase very carefully.*) I've just sold my own place, I'm moving on – so I'm sorting through everything I've got.

Julie   Still tidying! You always used to tell us tidiness was so important.

Minken   Exactly, I'm making sure I know where everything is – so I can find it when I really need it. (*He turns sharply.*) So this is magnificent isn't it, seeing you two again.

Richard (*surprised by this*)   Right . . . we must get you a drink Mr Minken. What do you want?

Lambert *and* **Summers** *enter.*

Minken   I think you'll find that that's been taken care of . . .

Summers *is carrying a large tray of drinks. She still has a very watchful manner and a sharp tongue.*

Julie   Miss Summers . . .!

Summers   We took the liberty of ordering a few drinks.

Lambert   I hope you don't mind. Just to start us off.

Julie   No, no that's very kind. (*To* **Summers**.) We can't shake hands obviously –

Summers   Take a drink, we can do all that stuff later! (**Julie** *peers at the drinks*.) There's red and white wine and vodka.

Julie   Vodka again?

Lambert   The drink of choice for this part of the evening. But of course we'll get you something else if you'd rather . . .

Julie   No, no. (*She takes a vodka and lime*.) Thanks.

Richard   I'll stick to my soft drink, for the moment. You look so well Miss Summers, just like Mr Minken.

Minken   They expected us to be so ancient!

Summers   Ah well, we weren't *that* old when we taught you.

Minken   One always expects one's ex-teachers to become very decrepit really quickly, every generation thinks that.

Richard   But you three clearly are not.

Minken   That is true.

He knocks back a vodka.

Summers   So, let me look at you properly. (*She gives them a beady stare*.) Richard . . . and Julie . . . who would have thought?!

Julie (*a little disconcerted*)   Who would have thought what?

Summers   That we'd ever see you again.

Richard   You both remember us as clearly as Miss Lambert does?

Summers   Of course.

Minken   Without question. So you two, what has become of you?

Momentary pause.

Julie   What has become of us?

Richard   You mean what are we doing now?

Summers   Precisely.

The three teachers stare at them.

Julie   Right . . . I work at a health practice, a group of four doctors . . . I am on reception . . . I've done that for seven years.

Lambert   Meeting every kind of person then?

Julie   All sorts, yes! I really enjoy it. And I have a partner, Dave – we're planning to have a baby, we're trying *vigorously* at the moment, every available opportunity . . . (*she smiles*) if that's not too much information.

Richard   Getting close Julie!

Minken   And you Richard?

Richard   Ah me . . .

Lambert   Ah you, yes.

Summers (*sharp*)   What's been happening to you Richard?

Richard   Well that's a tiny a bit complicated . . .

Minken   Give us just an impression.

Summers   The highlights.

Richard   An impression of my career? Not easy.

Lambert   Just a quick sketch Richard. Have a go. Now.

Richard   A quick sketch of my life?!

Pause.

Well, I'm married, to Grace, we bought a house, huge mortgage, but it's OK. We have a son, Leo, I hold him as much as I can, smell him as a baby – that fantastic smell, he's seven now. The house is a mess of course –

Summers (*sharp*)   I can imagine.

Richard (*straight back at her*)   And all the time I'm zigzagging between jobs . . . sixteen different jobs in five years, trying not to be found out. Although my reading and spelling is much better, thanks to all of you – I always have to have a strategy . . .

Minken   And are you found out?

Richard   My voice rescues me, I find my voice is my fortune. I start on help lines – I'm great on those because I don't stammer and sound very reassuring apparently. Somebody says you would be terrific in market research – so I'm out and about with a clipboard. Fast food, politics, what would you like on your mobile phone? I do them all! Complete strangers like you very much I'm told –

So suddenly I'm with a firm that does a lot of polling for the government and Number 10 – and on occasions I'm giving presentations to a room which includes the Chancellor of the Exchequer and the Home Secretary, and once or twice the Prime Minister himself. I get a close-up view of our leaders for several years, see how they drink in the polls – they go amazingly quiet. And today I'm working for another consultancy that does a lot of business with the top firms – using my voice to find things out.

And it's good. That's my life.

He looks across at them.

Lambert   It sounds like you're doing very well Richard.

Minken   Lecturing to the Prime Minster!

Richard   Yes, I think so. I've managed not to be rumbled – so far anyway – which is the main thing. (*He smiles.*) And of course I'm crammed with useless facts –

Julie (*suddenly firm*)   That's more than enough about us Richard. Quite enough. (*She turns.*) What about you three?

Minken   What do you want to find out?

Richard   You spend every night together do you?

Summers (*sharp*)   You really think that's likely?

Lambert   We'd go mad very quickly.

Summers   Besides Mr Minken has a wife . . .

Julie   But you see a lot of each other, don't you, visit each other's houses?

Richard   Crowd around the TV together, watching the latest reality show?!

Lambert   I hardly think so, they wouldn't come to watch TV in my house.

Minken   For years and years – until very recently – she had a black and white set.

Richard   A black and white TV?! That's brilliant Miss Lambert, perfect, you watching all the current celebrities just in black and white!

Minken   I rage at the TV anyway, I can't bear to watch those idiotic competitions.

Summers   Everybody humiliating themselves . . .

Julie   So what goes on when you meet, if you're not watching her black and white TV?

Richard   You watch her set off on her walks instead?

Julie   Maybe you go with her sometimes?

Minken   No, we don't.

Richard   So what really happens on your night walks Miss Lambert?

Lambert   I'm not sure I should tell you.

Richard   Blimey, what does that mean?

Lambert   It means what it says, that it's probably not a good idea that you learn about what I see.

Julie   Learn about? We aren't still seven years old!

Lambert (*smiles*)   No, but I wouldn't want to scare you.

Richard   Scare us?! How? That isn't possible Miss Lambert.

Lambert (*calmly*)   I think it probably is.

Minken   She sees some amazing things. Not always of course – but some truly amazing things.

Summers   She comes back and tells us. Things one would never expect.

Pause.

Julie   Give us an example of something we would never expect.

Lambert   Something I've seen?

Richard   No. (*Sharp smile.*) Something that you did. That would scare us.

Lambert   That *I* did?

Minken   There is quite a lot to choose from.

Pause.

Lambert   Well one night I walked beneath the city treading on the electric rails of the tube as I went.

Julie (*startled*)   How did you do that?

Richard   That's not possible!

Lambert   Oh yes it is. It's 2.30 in the morning, I'm walking past Chancery Lane tube station, a woman who is having a smoke yells out at me, 'What's the time love?'

Summers *moves, standing in the shadows near her, as she did in the assembly.*

Lambert   She asks where I'm going and I tell her I don't sleep at night, I walk.

And then she says . . .

Summers (*as woman*)   That makes two of us. Want to come downstairs and see where *I* do it?

Lambert   So we go into the empty station, and down the escalator and onto the platform and there are these women in overalls, crawling along the line picking up litter.

Summers   The electric current is switched off for a few hours for us, but we have to be careful we don't lose track of time and suddenly the rails are live again . . . (*she laughs*) maybe I should start wearing a watch!

The line of lights on the floor glows more brightly.

Lambert   And we walk along the tunnel a little way, I am keeping right to the edge, and she says,

Summers (*teasingly*)   Come on, you can step on the rails love, you can walk on them, and nothing will happen!

Lambert (*stepping gingerly along the white lights*)   At first I can't bring myself to, even though I can see others doing it. And then like a dream, I'm actually walking on top of the rails, one foot on each, what would normally kill you!

And as we go, at each station, the nature of the litter changes, depending which part of London we're in . . .

Summers   Under Tottenham Court Road, which is where we are now, you always get the most condoms and the most hypodermic needles . . . and when we reach Oxford Circus, you'll see we get the most tourist trash, plastic police helmets being a real favourite.

Lambert   When we get near the great department stores like Selfridges and the shops by Bond Street it is suddenly upmarket litter, and we see – and I promise you this is true, we see jewellery glinting in the dust amongst the rails . . . and then from further down the line this voice screams at us – 'Come here!'

Minken (*rasping out*) Come here and look at what I've found . . .

He is upstage by the vent, his suitcase slightly open.

You will never guess what they've dropped this time!

Lambert   This portly man is on the platform of Lancaster Gate, one of the cleaners, and he is yelling at us to come and have a look. My guide calls –

Summers   We've already found a necklace . . . and an amethyst ring.

Minken (*with disgust*)   And they won't even have noticed they've lost it, it won't even have registered!

Lambert   And then he sees me –

Minken (*to* **Lambert**)   Doesn't this waste make you sick?! Some people are so filthy rich, have got so much, they just chuck it away . . . (*He moves.*) But come here and look at these, because even I haven't found anything like this before –

He is peering into his half-open suitcase.

These disgusting little dolls . . .

Lambert   And he is standing with these very disturbing dolls.

Minken   Three dolls with pink dresses, one of them has been decapitated and the other two have broad grins on their faces . . .

He produces three stuffed toys from his suitcase, elderly teddies, very battered.

(*As himself.*) This is as close as I can get to them tonight . . .
(*Then as the man.*) So you tell me how did they end up here?
How on earth could that happen?

Lambert   And he gives me one of the dolls to examine, the
one without the head, and as I'm doing so –

Minken (*sinister smile*)   Enjoying your visit are you?

Lambert   Of course. It is so interesting to be down here in
the middle of the night –

Minken   You don't want to stay here too long of course, you
don't want to lose track of time!

Lambert   Yes I won't stay too long . . .

Minken   Because they put the current back on at 3.45, and
then a train comes through looking for rats and pigeons,
with a marksman on board and he shoots the vermin.

Lambert   And suddenly it's a little frightening – I need to
get out of there. I say something ridiculous, like 'Thank you
so much for showing me your work', and then I run up the
stairs at Lancaster Gate. But of course the gates are locked
and I don't know how to get out! I have to run back down
and ask for directions –

Minken   You want to get out do you? So go along the
tunnel to Notting Hill Gate, right along there . . . but you'll
have to be quick . . .!

Lambert   And I set off along the tunnel thinking the
current could be switched on at any moment, but they
wouldn't let that happen, would they? I reach the next
station, and I'm clambering up as fast as I can to the surface,
and then I'm outside at last gulping big breaths . . . and
never has London air seemed so sweet.

Silence. The white lights along the floor shine less brightly.

Richard   I wish I had been down there with you, walking
along the line!

Julie   Yes, I have always wanted to do that since I was tiny – tip-toeing along the rails –

Richard   Walking through the innards of London, what a great way to see the city! (*Turns to* **Minken** *and his suitcase.*) And you still have your props Mr Minken I see, just like you did when you were up on stage during assembly –

Minken   Yes, well that's purely coincidence, it's because I'm in transit with this stuff . . . (*He shuts the suitcase with a sharp smile.*) But I hope you don't mind us using our old methods.

Summers   We still quite like them!

Julie   I would never have guessed you would be walking along electric rails at 2.30 in the morning Miss Lambert!

Summers   She has surprised you then . . .

Richard   But I don't know why you thought we would be scared, that wasn't what I would call terrifying.

Lambert   I said I wasn't going to tell you those stories, remember Richard.

Richard (*straight at her*)   I don't remember you saying that, no.

Summers (*taking another drink*)   How do you think three dolls in pink dresses ended up lying on the track?

Minken   To drop one by accident is possible, but three, it must have been deliberate.

Julie   Maybe they belonged to a girl who sentenced them to death under the wheels of a train . . . (*she smiles*) that's one way of dealing with dolls you've outgrown!

Minken   Children at night . . . yes. That's quite another thing of course, she comes across plenty of children at night.

Lambert   Yes I do.

Summers (*suddenly to* **Lambert**)   Tell them about the ghost.

Richard The ghost?

Julie You met a ghost?!

Minken She met something special.

Pause.

Lambert I don't believe in ghosts . . . never have (*lightly*) not even Titus Meredith . . .

Richard Of course you don't. But . . .?

Lambert *knocks back another vodka.*

Lambert (*casually*)   I meet many different kinds of young people when I walk.

One summer night something happened that I can't quite explain.

Minken None of us can.

Lambert That's all that happened.

Richard *Please.*

Momentary pause.

Lambert I was going down Glasshouse Street just off Piccadilly, a figure steps out of a doorway, a young woman, 'Excuse me, excuse me Miss, have you got some money? I need to get home and I need to make a telephone call.' She is about sixteen, pale and very pretty, but she is oddly dressed, wearing a heavy coat even though it's mid-summer.

I give her three pound coins. She stares at the money totally bewildered.

'What is this? I've never seen money like this!'

She literally just lets the coins drop out of her hand. I bend down to pick them up, when I turn back she is looking at me rather desperately.

'It's my father's birthday, I must be back in time for the meal, it would be awful if I was late, it would break his heart. I *have* to call him and tell him I'm coming.'

I take out my mobile phone – I still had one then. 'You can use my phone' I say.

She looks at the phone in my hand as if I'm mad, as if I'm playing a trick.

'What is that? You make it work!' she says. I'm startled of course,

I say 'Give me the number.'

She looks me straight in the eye and says 'Park 4039'.

Momentary pause. She looks at them.

Park 4039 is an area code of my childhood.

Julie (*quiet*)   Shit.

Lambert   'Park 4039, are you sure?' I say to her, 'How can that be?'

'You're wasting my time', she bursts into tears. 'You can't help me!'

And she turns and disappears towards Piccadilly.

I walk after her rather fast, trying to get another glimpse of her, but she's gone.

Pause.

Richard   That's no ghost! That was just a kid playing around, maybe she had seen an old movie –

Julie   And was trying to freak people! And just possibly you'd had a drink or two as well?

Lambert (*firmly*)   No Julie, I can promise you, I was completely sober.

Minken (*beady look*)   Park 4039, those old phone numbers had a bit of poetry about them didn't they? Frobisher 7878 . . . Bluebell 2166 . . . Gibbon 3535! (*He turns.*) But that wasn't the end of the matter was it Elizabeth?

Summers   Something infinitely stranger happened.

Julie   Great! What?

Lambert (*calmly*)   You won't believe it.

Richard   Won't I?

Lambert   One morning a little over a year later, at the end of the walk, the sun about to rise, it's around 6.15, I decide to phone Mr Minken, to meet for breakfast. I know I can ring that early, Mr Minken being a very early riser –

Minken   Always. Often an hour ahead of Mrs Minken.

Lambert   By this time I had given up carrying a mobile, for reasons I can't go into – so I find a phone box, the familiar smell of urine, I dial Mr Minken's number . . .

We hear the phone ringing through the speakers.

It rings for an unusually long time . . . I'm just about to hang up –

Summers *is standing upstage with her back to us.*

Lambert   And then it's answered. It's a female voice, rather upper class.

Summers (*softly*)   Park 4039.

Lambert   My heart starts beating . . . I must have misheard, 'Sorry what number did you say?'

Summers   Park 4039. Who is this calling?

Lambert   I say 'It's Elizabeth Lambert'. There is the sound of dance music in the background as if from a radio and the clink of glasses . . .

Summers   And who do you want to speak to?

Lambert   My heart is really pumping now, but I can't stop myself, 'Is . . . is your daughter there? Can I speak to her?'

Pause.

Summers   I am afraid that's not possible, not anymore, our daughter is dead.

Lambert   I . . . I'm so sorry, I didn't know . . . I didn't realise.

We hear the period phone click off.

And she was gone.

Silence.

Richard   Amazing! You dialled Mr Minken and you got Park 4039!

Julie   You were probably asleep, it was a dream. You had been walking all night, you fell asleep –

Lambert   It's not that easy to fall asleep in a phone box Julie, have you ever tried it?

Summers   Elizabeth got through to Mr Minken moments later –

Minken   She was in a state of shock, when she reached my flat she was still shaking.

Pause.

Richard   Well why not? I do believe it. So phone boxes have memories! The old technology dying, soon to be obsolete, suddenly tuning into the wires of the city, sending you back in time. Why shouldn't you be able to phone the past if one concentrates long enough? It won't be long before you can do it on a computer, time travel –

Julie   Like you did with us in assembly, playing those tapes – how the city used to be. You were conjuring up the past.

Richard   Yes, old London, full of smoke and ships!

What doesn't quite fit though was why she – whoever it was who answered the phone – is up at 6.15 in the morning clinking wine glasses and listening to dance music?

Lambert (*smiles*)   Who knows, maybe it is always cocktail hour in the past . . . Of course I probably did hallucinate the whole thing from lack of sleep.

Julie   Maybe an old sound you half heard on your walk, like a typewriter – the last one in London – suddenly set off something in your mind, and you remembered a story about a girl who was late, and you sort of summoned her up, a daughter hurrying home and then –

A young woman in a black dress is standing in the shadows upstage. **Julie** *spins round in surprise and shouts.*

Julie   Shit! Fuck!

The young woman is a **Waitress***. She has a more sophisticated chilly manner than the* **Waitress** *in Scene Two.*

Waitress   I have just come for the glasses.

Julie   I'm so sorry, I didn't see you there!

Richard   We were just in the middle of something. (*He smiles.*) She thought you were a ghost.

Waitress   Well I don't think I am . . . (*She moves to get the glasses.*) Excuse me . . . (*She stops to pick up one of the teddy bears.*)

Minken   Yes, that's mine.

Waitress   Nothing's allowed on the floor for security reasons, as I'm sure you must realise.

Minken   Of course (*holding teddy*) I can see how this could look suspicious.

Waitress (*sharply, indicating the suitcase*)   And any luggage must be kept right next to you, never left unattended. (**Minken** *moves closer to the suitcase.*) That's right, yes. Now can I get you more drinks?

Summers   Not just yet, we have a couple left here, thank you.

Lambert (*calmly*)   And she is worried if I drink anymore they won't believe what I say.

Waitress (*turning at exit*)   There are plenty of seats at the bar you know. You don't have to be right back here . . .

Summers   We like it here.

The **Waitress** *exits.*

Julie   I'm so sorry, yelling out like that. I was thinking about that poor girl desperate to reach her dad, to honour his birthday . . .

Lambert (*calmly*)   You see it does get to one.

Richard   But you saw something much scarier than that.

Lambert   You reckon?

Richard   You've already told us you have.

Minken   There is one in particular.

Lambert   I'm not sure I want to go into that.

Richard   You say you meet a lot of children at night – I think it is about one of them, a *real* child you saw, who had an effect on you.

Lambert   That doesn't narrow the field, that quite often happens.

Richard   Why don't you carry a mobile phone?

Pause.

Lambert   Ah . . .

Richard   You dropped a heavy hint just now, so you obviously wanted to be asked.

Julie   You want us to find out!

Lambert   It does begin with a phone, yes. Somebody calling out in the street, just like the girl, so you won't believe me.

Minken   But this time we have proof don't we.

Julie   Proof of what?

Momentary pause.

Lambert   Well I need a phone to do this. (**Summers** *slips a mobile into her hand.*) I'm walking south of the river one night, down Black Prince Road. Suddenly this voice shouts at me, 'Can you help me?' I turn, a woman is coming straight at me.

Summers (*holding a mobile in front of her*)   Please can I use your phone, it is very important, can I?

Lambert   But she is holding a phone in her hand, pointing it at me, she sees my confusion.

Summers   I need *your* phone, please. I have to have somebody else's phone. I need to call my son, he knows my number, he will never answer when he can see it is me. But he might just answer a number he doesn't recognise.

Please can I have your phone?

Lambert   Her tone is so urgent, I find myself handing it to her without a murmur.

Summers (*dialling furiously*)   I want to hear his voice so much, even for a moment, to know he is OK, it doesn't matter if he doesn't tell me where he is, just to hear him speak . . . (*She puts the phone to her ear.*) Please, please pick up!

Lambert   He doesn't answer.

Summers (*sadly handing the phone back*)   Thank you so much. It was kind of you to let me do this. He is called Callum, my boy. I haven't seen him for five months, his dad has seen him, but I haven't . . . sometimes I think I'll never hear from him again.

Lambert   And then she was off.

Summers (*suddenly turning up stage*)   If you see a thin boy with blond hair walking the streets, tell him to call his mum.

Lambert   And then she disappears back up Black Prince Road.

Minken *turns and opens his suitcase with a sharp flick.*

Julie   What else have you got in there Mr Minken?

Minken *takes his jacket off and then his tie.*

Richard   The jacket's off! I remember Mr Minken taking his jacket off – it always meant he was changing into somebody else.

Lambert   Three weeks later I'm walking down Southampton Street, just off the Strand, at about 1 in the morning. Leaning against the lamp post is a chunky boy of about 15 – in one hand he has a phone and he is texting, and in the other he has a gun.

Richard (*disbelieving smile*)   A boy with a gun, leaning on a lamp post? Right!

Lambert   It's obviously a toy gun or a replica, it must be surely.

Minken *takes an old Luger, a black metal fifties toy gun, almost life size, out of his suitcase.*

Minken   It was longer than this, but this is the closest I have got in here.

Lambert   You get used to seeing things at night around town that seem unlikely, but the blatant way the boy is standing there, it is very strange. (**Minken** *turns towards her with the gun.*) But he is not Callum because he is very chunky.

Minken (*as boy*)   What are you staring at? (*Glances at gun.*) Don't worry you'll read about this in the papers tomorrow and you'll be able to say, I saw that guy last night!

Lambert   Why would I read about you in the papers?

Minken   Why do you think?

He moves with the gun.

Minken   I've been up on a roof near the river – nice flat roof – watching people walking along . . . (*He aims gun.*) It was a kind of rehearsal for what I'm going to do tomorrow, which of those shapes down there I'm going to take out.

Richard   A London sniper, in his dreams! Is that what he was?

Minken (*waving gun*)   I get this into school, through the metal detector, no problem. They get the knives, they get the other guns, but they don't get this, never have! People think it's plastic, but it's a very light metal, you want to touch? (*Moving closer.*)

Lambert (*calmly*)   Not tonight, no.

Minken (*turns*)   How many CCTV cameras do you think there are in my school?

Lambert   Sixteen.

Minken   Sixteen! You must be crazy, no! There are eighty-seven cameras in our school, eighty-seven of them!

Julie   Sounds like what's happened at my old school – it's become a fortress.

Minken   I go all over the school with this gun, holding it. They don't stop me! You know why? There is nobody, not one *single* person, watching those screens!

And everywhere I go – that fucking place, my school seems to follow me! Because if you take the whole city, just think how many cameras are out there. I go past them all the time, I show them my face, I show them the gun, I leave bits of myself all over the city, a little piece more each night – it's like being on a giant billboard, they've got so many pictures of me!

Richard   A star of CCTV, that's one way of doing it!

Minken (*points with gun*)   And they haven't spotted me once!

Lambert   Right . . . they haven't?

Minken   So tomorrow you'll read about me, because it is time to stop being just a face on the screen. It is time for some real action.

Lambert   And with that, he is off down the street – and something possesses me, even though he is chunky, he can't be Callum, I reach for my phone –

I have kept the number the woman called just in case . . . I ring that number. (*She presses the phone.*) He keeps going down the street, it's not Callum, of course not.

Suddenly the phone rings in **Minken***'s pocket. He stops, as the boy, takes out the phone, then looks back at* **Lambert***.*

Minken (*menacing, moving towards her*)   *You* did that didn't you?! How did you get my number?

Lambert   Your mother used my phone to call you . . . and she asked me to keep a look-out.

Minken   My mother?

Lambert   Will you call your mum?

Minken   Why?

Lambert   She just wants to hear your voice, know you're OK.

Minken   Yeah, it's been a few months, I have been staying on a friend's floor.

Lambert   Even a text would do I'm sure. Some kind of message from you.

Minken   A text? No I'll do more than a text, I'll *see* her. I'll go round before the end of the week, for a visit.

Lambert   And then he disappears round the corner.

Slight pause.

Richard   And did he? Did he see her?

Lambert   Yes.

Julie You brought them together? That's great – is that the story?

Richard I have a feeling that's not the story, no.

Summers Not exactly, no.

Lambert He did go home. He did see his mother. They had three meals together. She cooked the first, he the second, she the third – that was the big meal, corn-on-the-cob, roast pork and ice-cream and raspberries.

After that meal he takes a hammer and hits her on the head with such force her skull is smashed instantly.

Julie Oh my god!

Richard He killed her? He killed his mother!

Lambert Yes. He then cut her up on the kitchen table and put her in three plastic rubbish bags. But after he'd done it, he made no attempt to hide her, he left the bags outside the front of the building with several pairs of her shoes lined up next to them.

Richard He wanted to be caught.

Julie Wait a minute – I need to know something. (*They look at her.*) I tend to take things literally as you know – so I have to ask this, did this kid really exist? Did you give him a message and after that he went home and cut up his mum? That happened?!

Lambert Yes.

Julie Definitely?

Summers Yes, and she spared you some details too.

Richard I remember a case now in the papers, a school boy and his mother and rubbish bags in Camden –

Lambert That's how I found out, I read about it in the press, except the child was not named for legal reasons, but I had a terrible feeling that it was him. (*She moves the phone* *around in her hand.*) And then my phone rings, and it's his voice, unmistakably.

Minken (*upstage, quiet*)   I went to see her and look what happened.

Lambert   I can't reply, absolutely don't know what to say. He tells me all about it, the last meal, the food they ate, suddenly hitting her with a hammer.

Minken   After I hit her, I put the TV on – it was Wimbledon tennis, lots of applause and the noise of the ball, and there I was staring at the head of my mum and all the blood everywhere. You know what the last thing she said to me was? She looked at me and said,

'I'm so glad you're here . . .'

Julie (*quiet*)   That's unbearable . . . 'I'm so glad you're here' and then he smashes her over the head.

Minken (*quietly*)   I don't know why I did it, I really don't know. Will you come and see me? *Please will you come?*

Lambert   But of course I don't. And then he texts me on the first day of the trial – 'Bad news, they are calling me Boy X, nobody is using my real name, nobody knows it is me who did it!' A few days later he texts me, 'Things are much better, I've got fans, loads of emails and loads of texts, people wanting to know me'. And then when he is found guilty – 'My name is out there, I'm no longer Boy X, I'm in the papers, I'm kinda famous, I really am!!' (*Momentary pause.*) After the trial everything goes quiet for a bit –

Her phone beeps. She stares at it.

And then he texts – I don't know how he can still have his mobile now they have put him away . . .

Minken (*softly*)   I am downstairs. Come and look.

Lambert   I don't go and look.

Julie   But he can't, he can't be downstairs!

Summers   Physically he's locked up, electronically he is everywhere.

Lambert   A few months later I'm watching Wimbledon –

Richard   In black and white of course.

Lambert   My phone rings.

The phone in her hand rings.

Minken (*as himself*)   That is her *actual* phone.

Summers (*going up to* **Lambert** *and taking the phone*) Afterwards she gave it to me . . .

Summers *stands on the other side of the stage from* **Lambert** *and holds up the ringing phone at the end of her outstretched arm.* **Lambert** *stares at it.*

The phone clicks onto answer phone.

Lambert   And suddenly there he is . . .

A boy's voice erupts out of the phone, crying, really heartfelt crying, amplified over the speakers.

Boy X VO   I can't stand it . . . I just can't stand it . . . why did it have to happen?

Please tell me . . . why it happened?!

Julie   Oh God . . . there he is!

The sobbing continues out of the phone. **Summers** *holds it up invitingly.*

Boy X VO (*sobbing uncontrollably*)   Talk to me . . . please talk to me . . . I need you.

Lambert   He is in such torment . . .

She moves towards **Summers**. *She stretches out her hand.*

Lambert   I'm about to answer it, to speak to him . . .

Her hand is about to touch the phone. The crying abruptly stops. The boy's voice comes flat and menacing out of the phone.

Boy X VO   You see you ought to have come and visited me . . .

You're going to wish you had.

The phone clicks off. Pause.

Lambert   And that is the last I ever heard of him.

Summers   Up to now.

Lambert   So that is why I don't have a mobile phone.

Minken   We paid a small fee to keep his voice, as a reminder. Eternal Voicemail, one can dial it whenever one wants.

Silence.

Julie   What a horrible story. Why on earth did he kill his mother?

Lambert   I don't expect we'll ever know . . . of course I often wonder what would have happened if I hadn't given him the message.

Minken   He would have done it anyway.

Lambert   Yes that is probably right.

Summers   Maybe a week later. He was always going to do it.

Richard (*suddenly*)   I can understand Boy X.

Summers   You can?!

Richard (*with authority*)   Yeah I believe so, yes. A mother that drives you mad, that always wants to know where you are, yet who shuts her eyes in embarrassment at your spelling, turns away in disgust when you stammer . . . Always makes you feel a problem . . . so you long for another identity, for a bit of stardom. (*Lightly, looking straight at* **Lambert**.) And then you meet someone else, elegant, friendly, imaginative, much better looking than your mum

– who makes you feel clever. Obviously an ideal substitute parent. Absolutely I can relate to him.

Lambert (*meeting his look*)   I was all that to him? I don't see how I can have been!

Julie   Well I can't recognise any of myself in him – not one bit – except maybe wanting to be on a giant billboard when I was ten years old.

Minken (*suddenly*)   It was that building that made him a monster of course.

Julie   The building?

Minken   Yes, how can you have a school that has 87 cameras? And metal detectors! How can that not be madness?

Summers   It is imbecilic, it is suicidal.

Minken   All those silent cameras are yelling at you! It's a war zone isn't it.

And so you go out at the end of the school day – and what have you become?

Summers   You've become Boy X, that's what you've become! The cameras watching, the metal detectors, the body searches!

Minken (*turns, his manner intense*)   What happened to the city of my youth? I was never afraid in London ever, not for one single day of my childhood, and I went all over, I roamed wherever I wanted.

Summers   I always felt safe. Always, always, always! *But not anymore!*

Summers *and* **Minken** *facing* **Richard** *and* **Julie**.

Julie   Well this is my home town too and I don't feel it's changed that much since I was small, it's not *that* dangerous.

Richard   It's one version of London Mr Minken, maybe, but not the only one.

Minken   No, something has died, something that I loved. It's lost all its graciousness, all its style, all its uniqueness. My city! How have we let that happen?

Silence. **Minken** *has turned away, by his suitcase.*

Richard   Are you alright Mr Minken?

Minken   Yes . . . (*Slight pause.*) I think I should try to show you something using what I've got here. It's a bit of a risk because it will seem rather odd –

Richard (*smiles*)   Maybe it's a little late for us to worry about that . . .

Minken (*opening the suitcase*)   But it's not as strange as it looks . . .

He rolls out, across the floor, the contents of the suitcase. Marbles, followed by old toys, cars, tanks, fire-engines, aeroplanes, buses and tractors.

Julie   Jesus Mr Minken! (*Trying to stop the marbles.*) They're going everywhere . . .

Richard   So that's what you were carrying!

Minken (*rolling the toy vehicles across the floor*)   Most of this is just worthless toys of course, marbles and Dinky cars, fighter jets, ice-cream vans –

Summers (*by the toys*)   Steam engines . . .

Lambert (*moving over*)   And even Greenline buses . . . The fifties and early sixties are here in miniature!

Minken (*rolling the last toys out*)   What my brother and I played with . . . there's even a little Sputnik amongst all this, the first moon rockets. And there are some earlier childhoods here too, like this 1930s flying boat . . .

Richard   And these ocean liners, this is the *Queen Mary*!

It's a beautiful collection Mr Minken.

Minken   Yes. Everything here just comes from department stores of the time, nothing special at all. (*He moves away from the toys.*) But even when I was outgrowing them I knew they would be worth preserving.

And if you look at them – what really hits you? (*His tone very forceful.*) I tell you what hits me – nothing has any innocence anymore does it?! Not like this!

Richard (*picking up a toy*) Maybe these US tanks aren't wholly innocent?

Minken   I don't know, even those Cold War toys have a certain charm now, at least you had to create your own game with them. There *was* an innocence then even though it was a dangerous time in the world. (*He turns away from the toys sharply.*) But yes nostalgia is extremely unwise of course, I agree.

Summers   And we were never nostalgic about the past.

Lambert   I never taught like that.

Minken   No, we were never trapped in the past. Far from it.

He faces **Julie** *and* **Richard***, a sharp smile.*

So let's take this place . . . where you're standing now shall we instead?!

Julie   'Take it'? In what way?

Minken (*his tone sharp, penetrating*)   You think you know this place do you? This mall?

Richard   Well I've been here a couple of times, yes, though never I admit to level zero four.

Minken   You think you're in a bar in the bowels of a shopping mall and there are shops and restaurants with soft lights and cinemas all around? And it's huge, and a little impersonal, but at least it's all of a piece. (*Sharp intense.*) Is that what you think?!

Julie (*apprehensively*)   That's what we think, yes.

Minken   But you couldn't be more wrong . . .

He moves deliberately across the stage, and then with a flourish he throws open the emergency exit, a door in the back wall we haven't noticed before. An orange light blazes out of it.

Julie   Fuck! Where does that lead to?!

Minken (*indicating beyond the orange light*)   Go down this exit, down to the car park this way, and you can get very scared, a world of pipes and metal staircases and a strange hum, where people are lurking to see which cars they are going to break into, or dealing in drugs . . . or just watching you.

Behind these shop fronts there is a terrifying world . . . (*A sharp smile.*) Must be time to leave town mustn't it?! (*He turns in the orange light.*) I should show you now . . . what lies beneath! Want to come?

Suddenly the overhead lights come on, a bank of high fluorescence. The space is revealed in stark brilliant white light. All the toys over the floor, the marbles everywhere.

The **Waitress** *standing staring at them.*

Waitress   What on earth do you think you're doing? The general public are not allowed to open that door . . .

Minken   I'm sorry. I was just demonstrating something to them.

Waitress   Shut it immediately. It can only be opened in an emergency.

Minken *obediently shuts the door. The characters caught in the brilliant white light stare at the waitress.*

Waitress   And what is all this on the floor?

Lambert   Mr Minken was just illustrating what he was saying to us, using what he happened to have in his luggage.

Minken   I'm very sorry, I got carried away. I will clear it all up now, absolutely.

Waitress   Well none of us are going to do it, that's for sure. (*Nudging the marbles with her foot.*) And every one of these have to be found, somebody could do themselves an injury.

Julie   We'll all help clear up.

Waitress   Yes, well you better start, because I don't want to have to call security.

The **Waitress** *exits.*

Minken (*to* **Julie** *and* **Richard**)   My deep apologies, I got too excited . . .

They all start to pick up the marbles and toys under the white light.

Richard (*on all fours, picking them up*)   No, no need to apologise Mr Minken . . . it was great to see these things . . . and I never expected at the start of the evening to be crawling around picking up toys for my ex-teachers.

Minken   Yes, that is a surprise I can see that. You must allow me to make up for this, I insist you let me cook supper for both of you tonight.

Richard   Tonight?

Minken   Yes, a quick supper for all of us. Please spare the time. It's the least I can do. Will you come?

Lambert   Mr Minken is one of the finest cooks I've ever met.

Summers   And that's no exaggeration. (*Sharp.*) Of course you may have more important things to do.

Julie   No, I think a quick meal will be nice – if that is I can get the image of Boy X and his mother and their last meal out of my head.

Richard We'll come.

Minken Good. Perfect. And I think we've picked up everything. (*He drops a toy into the suitcase with a sharp smile.*) That's the last fire-engine . . .

Julie I have my car in the car park . . . on one of the higher levels, not quite so sinister there! I need to get it out before it costs me fifty quid. (*To* **Minken**.) Can I give you a lift or do you have your car?

Minken No, we'll come with you.

Summers And then we can show you the way.

Richard And I will take Miss Lambert.

Lambert You don't need to do that, there'll be room in their car, or I can find my own way.

Richard Don't be absurd, of course we should go together.

Minken Right . . . (*He begins to move off with his heavy suitcase,* **Julie** *and* **Summers** *following him.*) In this light it all looks different doesn't it?!

They exit. **Lambert** *and* **Richard** *alone. Silence.*

Richard So you tell ghost stories now.

Lambert Only one was a ghost story.

Richard You tell spooky stories instead of the time-travelling ones that inspired me when I was little.

Lambert Yes.

Richard Why?

Lambert Because that is what I see. I warned you they were unsettling didn't I . . . a little frightening.

Richard And you rather enjoy telling scary stories don't you?

Lambert It depends. I don't do it that often.

Richard   You're still wonderful.

Lambert (*she laughs*)   Wonderful? That's not true.

Richard   A wonderful storyteller. You know you were the first person in the world to show me there was such a thing as the past.

Lambert   Well I was your first teacher, so that's no surprise.

Richard   I can still remember what it felt like when I was small and alone with you. I was very nervous, almost terrified.

Lambert   Terrified? Surely not?

Richard   Almost terrified. Certainly at first, before our lessons together began to work. But at the same time I was very excited, I knew it was a real privilege to be alone with Miss Lambert.

Lambert   You were very tiny, so you don't remember it right.

Richard   I wasn't that tiny. And I do remember it right.

Lambert   And now?

Richard (*looks straight at her*)   Not terrified of course, but very nervous, certainly.

Lambert   Really Richard?

Richard   There is a gulf here obviously, because you were such a huge thing in my life when I was a boy – and I, to you, was just one of the thousands of kids you've taught over the years.

Lambert   That's right.

Richard   I remember you, I have pictures in my head of you, I think about you often, and yet you are a complete stranger now.

Lambert Of course I am, you were 14 when we last saw each other.

Richard Why are you walking around the city at night?

Lambert Because that's what I find myself doing.

Richard That's no kind of answer.

Lambert I think it's a very good answer. (*She moves.*) There's another marble . . .

She bends down and picks up a marble.

I don't like too many questions Richard, (*she smiles*) even from an ex-pupil like you . . .

She is standing with her back to him.

Richard Of course. But I'm going to find out more Miss Lambert.

Lambert (*not facing him, but her voice is light*) Are you Richard?

Fade.

Act Two

THIRD ASSEMBLY

The back wall is in darkness. Just a single pool of light downstage. There is the sound of children's voices, chattering and laughing, building to a crescendo. Then suddenly they fall silent all at once, an expectant hush.

Lambert *enters, into the pool of light, wearing a summer dress.*

Lambert   Good morning everyone.

The children's voices chorus back 'Good morning Miss Lambert'.

Today we are going to do something I've never done before.

We're going to try to time travel at night.

She looks at us.

So let's choose a night shall we. When will it be? Maybe a good time to choose is the middle of the nineteenth century around 1860, when Queen Victoria was on the throne. (*She moves slightly and smiles.*) And when we've travelled there, I will tell you who amongst you made this possible. Because one of you sitting here made this happen.

So what would you have heard if you had been alive at that time? If you'd climbed out of your bed on a summer night and stood at your bedroom window and stared out across London?

Of course there would have been the sound of all those horse-drawn carriages and hansom cabs . . .

City soundscape of the past ringing around us.

And maybe by now, after all the time-travelling assemblies we've done you're expecting that and can imagine it easily . . .

The sounds die away except one clock striking.

But as you stand there in your pyjamas or nightdress, there is another sound you might have heard that would have made you press right up to the windowpane in excitement.

And it is this.

We hear the sound of distant roars.

The roars and cries from the animals of the jungle travelling towards you through the night air. And these sounds are not just from the Zoo in Regent's Park, not by any means.

Because if you had opened that window in front of you, and suddenly flown out of it, like Peter Pan did, across the roof tops of the city, what would you have discovered?

If you had flown west you would have heard the roars of the circus lions from their cages near the Princess Louise pub in Fulham, and then if you had taken a sharp turn and flown north, you would have heard the trumpeting of the elephants which were kept near Camden Lock, Queen Victoria's own personal elephants that had been given to her as a gift.

And then if you had flown east towards the Docks, towards Tobacco Road and Artichoke Hill, you would have heard the sounds of literally hundreds of different animals – for this is where Jamrach's Exotic Emporium was, the biggest pet shop in the world. Tigers growling, monkeys screeching, 50 parrots calling.

The sound of the animals' cries building.

These were the extraordinary sounds you might have heard from your bedroom as you stared out . . . on a still night the city shook with the cries of exotic animals.

It would have been a little frightening at first of course, but how dramatic too, don't you think?

As you get back into bed, the sound of roaring lions fills your dreams. A Victorian summer night, not what you – or I – were expecting. Not at all.

And that idea was Richard Kenton's. He is doing a special project on circuses and on Queen Victoria's elephants . . . and it was he who thought of flying over the city, and hearing all the different animals! That was Richard's imagination. But he wanted me to present it.

I hope I did it well enough Richard.

Blackout.

The sound of the animals rise to a crescendo and then cut out abruptly, as the sound of a tube train rumbles past.

Scene One

Minken's *basement flat. There are a couple of old-fashioned wooden filing cabinets and a large dark cupboard standing against the back wall. There are a few severe-looking high-backed wooden chairs.*

It is the same night. **Summers** *is sitting on one of the high-backed chairs smoking.* **Julie** *and* **Richard** *are across from her. The light is very low. The sound of a tube train dying away.*

Julie   Jesus I'm full . . . that was an amazing omelette!

Summers   Mr Minken takes his cooking very seriously, even more so since his retirement. And of course there's pudding still to come . . .

Richard (*suddenly getting up*)   You don't think we might have a little more light?

It's rather sepulchral in here isn't it.

Summers   It's best not to touch anything. But I'm sure you can ask him and see what he says.

Richard   Right. (*He smiles.*) The lights coming on have to be negotiated do they?!

Julie (*looking around*)   Not many pictures are there, or family photos. There's nothing personal. He must obviously really like the tube too . . . living this close to it.

Richard   Yes, you always expect to be above the tube – but we seem to be right next to it.

Summers (*blows smoke*)   Mr Minken likes to be private.

Richard   And subterranean! (*He moves around the darkened flat.*) When you're little you never imagine teachers having homes do you, having front doors that they disappear through at the end of the day. You think they must live at the school somehow, in grand rooms you never see, looked after by the dinner ladies.

Minken *enters with* **Lambert**. **Minken** *is holding a tray with fluted glasses on it. There is a portion of raspberry jelly in each one. There is also a plate of sponge fingers on the tray and a jug of custard.*

Minken   Pudding is up!

Lambert   What on earth are you doing sitting in the dark?

Minken (*putting down tray, turning more lights on*)   Yes, we can't have that! Need to see what we're eating.

Richard   Jelly and custard?

Minken   And sponge fingers. The old puddings are always the best. Everybody who wants one, take one.

Julie (*taking a jelly*)   You can't have made this tonight. Do you have a fridge full of jelly?

Richard   Just waiting for old kids that you used to teach to drop by?

Minken   No, I make a lot for myself. Especially while my wife is away, I find it soothing. She's on a visit to Australia.

Summers (*tucking into jelly*)   There's always enough to eat here.

Lambert   School food, but it is great school food – taken to another level entirely.

Minken   My son's become a chef at a small restaurant, he's followed my cooking sadly, rather than my teaching!

Julie (*eating*)   It's funny how jelly takes you right back doesn't it, from the first spoonful . . .

Richard *is by one of the filing cabinets, pulling open one of the drawers.*

Minken (*very sharp*)   Don't touch! Please!

Richard *turns, very startled.*

Minken   I'm sorry, but please don't touch.

Richard   I apologise. I didn't mean to pry –

Minken   I know where everything is in the room you see. How it's filed.

Lambert (*eating a spoonful of jelly*)   And he gets a little edgy if that is disrupted in any way.

Richard   Where everything is filed? Does that mean you've got all sorts of things from the past here?

Julie   From when we were little? Have you?

Minken (*slight pause*)   You're asking me if I've kept things?

Richard   Yes.

Minken   Keeping too much from the past is of course a well-known taboo among those that teach.

Richard   Really? I didn't know that. I've never heard that before.

Julie   I think you've just made that up.

Richard   What about the toys in your suitcase?!

Minken   The toys are different.

Summers (*suddenly*)   Show them the drawings. That can do no harm.

Pause. Then **Minken** *approaches the large cupboard.*

Minken Obviously every child paints, in every school that's ever existed. And over just a few years that quickly amounts to thousands and thousands of pictures. Most go home with the child of course, but on occasions the pictures are too big to take home – usually the ones they have worked on together. (*He half opens the cupboard door.*) It may seem strange – but instead of them becoming rubbish, or being burnt . . .

Lambert He kept the best.

Minken I began to make my own selection.

Minken *opens the cupboard. We see rolls and rolls of paper, bound and stacked, some large rolls, some short.*

Minken And though I'm clearing everything out, I do still have them. (*He stares at the rolls for a moment.*) And sometimes the best coincided with something big happening in the world.

Summers Something they'd be told to notice.

Lambert And which then fired their imagination, those are the ones he kept.

Minken *pulls out one of the largest rolls.*

Minken Can you take the other end Geraldine?

Summers *and* **Minken** *begin to uncoil the roll. It is at least four feet wide and fifteen feet long. They hold the picture.*

Richard That is a big picture!

Minken This is a really easy one to guess, what great event it shows . . .

The large scroll of paper is covered in sunflowers, large sunflowers and small, drawn by different children, and among the flowers people's faces singing and shouting. And among the faces a collage of actual objects stuck on the painting, party hats, party streamers, pieces of balloons and glitter and ice-cream cones made out of cardboard, and real crisp packets, and then more painted sunflowers.

Minken   Guess!

Richard *and* **Julie** *stare at it.*

Julie   It's probably screamingly obvious to most people, but I haven't a clue.

Minken   You really don't know?

Lambert   Maybe it's because you've only got half way.

Minken   Oh yes . . .

They unroll the wall of sunflowers and sweets further. There is a gap in the middle; the wall has been split in two.

Richard   A hole in the wall! Of course, it's the fall of the Berlin Wall!

Lambert   Yes, the kids made this enormous wall that burst with sunflowers.

Julie   And ice-cream and crisp packets!

Lambert   Yes, it was prophetic too, with bits of McDonalds cartons – see here – being stuck to it, what was going to spread like a plague. Everything they loved at that time they put on the wall.

Richard   I can see why you kept it . . . a terrific record of what kids really craved.

Julie   Ah there's E.T. crawling up the side of the wall here . . .

Lambert   But the sunflowers were entirely their idea. (*She walks along the painted wall.*) All the schools that month had pictures that burst with colour.

Summers (*dryly*)   When the world seemed to be buzzing with possibilities. We pinned this up outside our staff room, marking the end of the Cold War. (**Minken** *and* **Summers** *pin it up along the back wall.*) It greeted us every morning.

Richard   The children's version!

Minken *takes another picture from the cupboard.*

Minken   Have a go at this one now. It's the easiest big picture I've got.

Minken *and* **Summers** *unroll a huge reclining figure, starting at the feet, bright red shoes with gold buckles. The female figure is lying in a field surrounded by rolling pins and a crown, tall red flowers, some of which turn into brambles which are twisting round her body.*

Richard (*as the picture unfurls*)   The Wizard of Oz . . . and a touch of Sleeping Beauty . . . a sprinkling of Snow White . . .

Julie   It's the death of Diana, surely?!

Lambert   That's right . . . all those fairy stories their parents had told them, and I had told them, coming together with her death . . .

Minken *and* **Summers** *pin the picture up.*

Julie   This is not all their own work is it? It can't be?!

Summers   I drew the outline for them, but they told me what to do. They supplied all the details very definitely, like the brambles beginning to cover her.

Minken   Geraldine helped with the art, but she didn't *make* the art.

Summers   And in our school, the way Elizabeth ran it, the kids' imaginations were always being stretched. There was always a little bit of mystery.

Julie   Well I can see why they were difficult to take home, they're enormous!

Minken   Yes, I was left with the gigantic pictures . . . but also the pictures that nobody wanted to take home.

He reaches into the cupboard and takes out two smaller pictures. He begins to unroll the first one.

Summers   Because they found them disturbing.

Minken   And the disturbing ones were often the most interesting of course, like this from the first Gulf War in 1991. The oil fields burning, everything just smoke and flames – what they'd picked up from the TV and transformed.

And then of course there's 9/11.

He shows the second picture.

Lambert   The twin towers lying down in coffins of their own, giant coffins for each building.

Summers   I didn't help them at all with that one, this is all the way they saw it. A few weeks later they went back and stuck autumn leaves all over the picture. (*She pins it up.*)

Julie   It's beautiful that one. I'm surprised no one wanted to keep it.

Richard (*staring at the display*)   History in children's pictures, it's great isn't it!

(*Animated.*) You know I've never thought, not for a single moment, about what happened to all those projects at school that weren't taken home. Of course they had to go straight in the bin – or all schools would just grind to a halt wouldn't they, become completely gummed up. But there had to be somebody somewhere who had the idea of keeping them, preserving the most telling, and it was you Mr Minken! That's a terrific thing to do.

Minken   I thought so, yes. A worthwhile thing. And I only kept the absolute best.

Julie   There can't be many people who have ever done that can there?!

Summers   Frederick likes to keep things.

Minken   My first pick was a picture done for the Jubilee in 1977 – the Queen Mother as a giant otter.

Richard (*staring at the pictures displayed*)   And all this coming out of a little school in north London . . .

Summers   Yes, they measure our time there. (*Sharp.*) He didn't just keep pictures though.

Julie   Right? (*To* **Minken**.) So what else have you got then? (*She smiles.*) You've got to show us!

Lambert   He's got tapes. Recordings. All beautifully labelled of course.

Richard   The Minken tapes!

Summers   And each has their own little box.

Minken *has opened one of the filing cabinets.*

Minken   Yes, these are *audio* tapes only. There was quite enough videoing from the parents.

Richard   Are these the sounds you played us in assembly?

Julie   If I heard those now, I don't know . . . I'll shrink back to a six-year-old probably.

Minken   I have those yes – but I have other things as well . . . (*He opens a drawer and peers in.*) What will it be? (*He examines the contents of the drawer.*) As you can see I broke the teachers' taboo rather seriously. (*He shuts the drawer, having taken something out.*) The earliest tapes, those from the seventies, are rather fragile . . . but here's one I can play. (*He pushes a cassette into a tape recorder.*) I've kept this for a number of reasons. It is from the autumn of 1990.

Summers   Around the time Mrs Thatcher was falling.

Minken   A concert . . . a school orchestra.

Lambert   We prided ourselves on our music back then.

We hear the sound of a small orchestra playing a piece of baroque music.

Minken   Some of the teachers were playing as well, including myself. I am one of the violas. So it is quite a full sound.

Julie   Music and pictures from when we were tiny!

Richard   Suddenly we'll be sitting on those little plastic chairs again . . .

Lambert (*standing by the pictures on the back wall*)   I'll tell you what's really interesting about these pictures.

Richard (*lightly*)   Yes Miss Lambert?

Lambert   When the children start school the parents are absurdly proud of any pictures they do. *Any* painting, however bad – a green orange, a tomato shaped like a carrot – is displayed in triumph on the walls of their home. But as soon as which school they are going to next beckons – the parents completely lose interest in any painting they do.

Julie   My mum never wanted to see any of my pictures, even at the tomato-shaped carrot stage.

Minken *winds on the tape. A boy begins to sing a solo.*

Richard   What a great voice this kid has got!

Julie   Yeah, that's a glorious sound . . .

Richard   Of course you'd keep something like this.

Minken   It was a good vintage that year, the little orchestra . . . the singers, they were particularly fine. (*The boy's golden voice singing in the background.*) Do you want to hear something rather funny?

Richard   Something rather funny Mr Minken, of course.

Minken   This boy . . . (*He indicates the sound.*) The boy with the magical voice here, do you know what happened to him? (*A momentary pause.*) Of course you don't, how could you! I will tell you.

He was one of the prime movers in the banking crisis of 2008, he helped to completely destroy his bank.

The beautiful innocent voice continues to sing.

Julie   Blimey!

Summers   Singing like an angel here – losing trillions a few years later.

Richard   This kid here?! Are you sure about that?

Minken   Completely. It's quite funny don't you agree?! I love it how this voice turned into that man. (*He winds on the tape again.*) And now . . . this voice? What happened to him?

A second voice has begun a solo, another beautiful unbroken male voice.

This boy here, with a truly heavenly voice, a few years later was done for armed robbery and attempted murder. He went to jail for fifteen years.

He's about a third of the way through his sentence at the moment.

Julie   Oh come on!

Richard   I don't believe you Mr Minken!

Minken (*suddenly very sharp*)   You don't believe me?

Lambert   Frederick is never wrong.

Richard   No, I don't believe you. It can't be an orchestra and choir made up entirely of lost souls – that's ridiculous! (*Sharp smile.*) There must be a few future doctors in there, a chiropodist at least.

Lambert   Of course not all the kids from this particular year turned out badly, what would that say about our teaching after all?!

Minken (*icily, to* **Richard**)   I don't remember what happened to every single child, obviously. That is impossible.

No doubt there is a future doctor in there somewhere . . .
(*Pointedly.*) And you, as a professional pollster, will know what
the percentages are likely to be.

I was just talking about what happened to the soloists – and
what became of them I think is very interesting. (*He stops the
music with a sharp movement.*) But since you don't believe me,
there is no point showing you any more, you're quite right.

Julie   No, don't stop now –

Richard   Please, I'm sorry, I didn't mean to insult you.

Minken   You said you don't believe me! Do you think I
made it up?

Richard   No, of course not, only that maybe you were
exaggerating . . .

Minken *begins to roll up one of the pictures on the wall.*

Lambert   Mr Minken doesn't tend to exaggerate.

Richard   Please, you must go on with your tapes!

Julie   What other things have you got in your cupboard?
Come on Mr Minken –

Minken   No, no, as I said you are quite right, I ought to
stop. You reminded me what I should be doing, what I've
had to do every day for many months now . . . (*he holds one
of the small pictures*) which is taking part of what I've collected
– including the children's pictures – like these autumn leaves
after 9/11 and doing this with it . . .

*He switches on a shredder which has been lurking in the corner. It's
green light shines out.*

Julie   You're going to shred it for fuck's sake?! After
keeping it all this time!

Minken   This flat has been sold. Everything has to be
sorted and moved. My collection is too big.

Minken *advances on the shredder with the picture.*

Richard   You can't do that! I'll take it home, if you've suddenly not got space for it.

Minken (*stopping with picture above shredder*)   You would keep it would you?

Julie   Yes, of course he would. If he doesn't, I will.

Richard   Certainly I'll keep it, it's a unique view of the past.

Julie   We'll take bundles if necessary, if you want us to –

Minken   I don't think so. (*Holding the picture up.*) You really think this would look right in your house? After one week in your home –

Summers   It would go straight in the bin.

Julie   It wouldn't!

Lambert   You want to wake up to that every morning? Mr Minken is right, I don't think you do.

Minken (*pulling autumn leaves off*)   Somebody else's child's picture, it wouldn't last.

Minken *shreds the picture.*

Julie   Oh no!

Richard   I wish you hadn't done that.

Minken (*watching the picture being shredded*)   Forgive a rather obvious statement, but this is my collection – my professional life is here! (*He picks up a piece of the shredded picture.*) I'm making a selection I can take with me, because I'm leaving town. I promised my wife I would have this done by the time she returns. (*He carefully collects the shredded fragments.*) I've left the pictures to last.

Richard (*pause*)   He is right of course, we don't have any connection with these . . .

Summers   No, you don't.

Minken (*indicating shredder*)   If I leave it, I will get behind. I haven't nearly done today's quota yet.

He picks another picture out of the cupboard.

Richard   Won't the neighbours mind the noise? It's nearly 1 in the morning.

Minken   I've had no complaints so far. (*More emollient.*) I will do this small one next, which you haven't seen.

He shreds the next picture.

Julie   Well even if nobody can hear it, I don't think I want to watch kids' pictures being shredded in the early hours! (*She picks up her bag.*) So I think it's time to . . .

Minken   Yes of course, it is late for you I understand.

Summers   Past her bedtime . . .

Lambert (*suddenly*)   We haven't had coffee though.

Richard   Coffee? (*To* **Lambert**.) Does that mean you are asking us to stay?

Lambert   I just thought I would mention Mr Minken makes an exceedingly good cup of coffee.

Blackout.

We hear the sound of the shredder, its sound amplified over the speakers, with its green light shining. After a few seconds it blends into the children's singing, the two soloists together, and then the whole choir of children.

Scene Two

The sound of the singing and the music cuts out suddenly. **Minken**'s *flat. There is a pool of light coming from stage right, as if from a kitchen. The children's pictures on the wall have all gone; dominating the room now are sacks, large plastic see-through rubbish bags of shredded paper, the shredded children's pictures.*

Lambert *and* **Julie** *are alone.* **Julie** *is smoking.*

Lambert   Any moment.

Julie   Any moment what?

Lambert   Any moment the solitary train that runs in the small hours –

Julie   The one they shoot rats off?

Lambert   The rat train yes, we should hear it very soon.

It sounds different from the other trains.

Julie (*ironic laugh*)   Wow! Worth waiting up for is it?

Lambert   Absolutely. I find it rather soothing in fact.

Julie   You would! Mind you . . . (*She stares at the sacks of shredded pictures.*) Something soothing would be good. It was really quite upsetting watching these being destroyed. (*She sinks her arm into one of the sacks.*) We'll never know what else was here will we . . .

Lambert   He can't keep everything. He has made that clear.

Julie   Of course not. But what he showed us was beautiful, and now most of it's gone.

Lambert   Frederick's intensity as a teacher was something very unique, his collection is a reminder of those days – maybe it's a little too vivid a reminder.

Julie   Is his wife really coming back from Australia?

Lambert   Oh yes. They are not breaking up, if that's what you mean, that's not why he is doing this.

Julie (*suddenly looking across at her*)   You know Elizabeth . . . (*She stops.*) I'm going to call you Elizabeth because I have never called you that before.

Lambert   Please do, you should have started long ago.

Julie   Right. It's surprisingly difficult to say as it happens. (*She turns.*) Elizabeth I think you should leave, get away from here right now.

Momentary pause.

Lambert   Before Mr Minken's coffee?

Julie   Before Mr Minken's coffee, yes. I'll drive you home.

Lambert   Why should I leave now, before the coffee? It doesn't make sense.

Julie   Because . . . this isn't easy either . . . (*She stops.*) Because I hate seeing you like this.

Lambert   Like what Julie? (*Very calm.*) What do you mean?

Julie   What you've become.

Lambert (*with sound of the subterranean train approaching*)   Ah here she comes.

The rumbling sound gets loud and close

(*Smiles.*) It's just a few feet from us really. It is a different colour from the other trains too, it is a garish green. And it is pulling an open carriage, with a marksman who wears a rather fetching red baseball cap – the wrong way round of course –

Julie   Don't change the subject.

Lambert (*nonchalantly*)   Did I? I apologise. I thought you'd want to know about the green train and the marksman.

Julie (*suddenly sharp*)   You must realise what effect you're having. You helped me Elizabeth! I took everything so literally, I was completely lost, and you gave me a way out of that. But sometimes I get like that still – like right now. I see you here in the early hours of the morning in this spooky flat, with Mr Minken shredding his collection – and you know what, I take that situation very literally.

Lambert   Well I can understand it's a little unsettling for you Julie, you see a woman staying up all night most nights, somebody who you think ought to know better –

Julie   I'm not being that literal. I see a little more than that!

Lambert Which is?

Julie Somebody who clearly isn't very happy.

Lambert Not very happy? Oh Julie, that's not what this is about.

Julie I don't believe you.

Lambert Right.

Silence.

Julie Love?

Lambert Yes?

Julie Tell me about love Elizabeth.

Lambert Tell you about love? That's a little ridiculous isn't it, I know you're in love Julie, and trying for a child –

Julie Longing for a child, yes.

Lambert And that's splendid naturally, but it doesn't mean that I –

Julie Have you ever been in love?

Lambert Of course. There have been moments all through my life.

Julie Right . . . (*She moves.*) I remember you telling us about a dog and a bird being in love and them both barking at each other – that stayed with me all this time.

Lambert I'm glad to hear it. (*She smiles.*) But I don't think any of my relationships were quite that strange.

Julie Who were you in love with?

Lambert Various people. I had one great love affair that lasted on and off for eighteen years. He was a history lecturer called Robin. He died young, a little while ago now.

Julie And children?

Lambert   I almost had a child with him, but in the end the school was all consuming and I decided against it.

(*She looks across at her.*) This isn't about love and losing it Julie, this isn't about loneliness.

Julie   No? Here's a woman walking through the city every night on her own until dawn – what the fuck is that, if it's not about being lonely, wanting to meet someone? –

Lambert   But I'm not Julie. That is where you are completely wrong.

Julie   I think you should come away with me now.

Lambert   I can't leave at this stage of the evening, it's not what happens.

Julie   What do you mean it's not what happens?! It can if you want it to.

Lambert   It's not what is going to happen because my friend and colleague of many years is packing up his flat, an emotionally difficult thing for him to do, and tonight I'm keeping him company. I'm not leaving before what's going to happen has happened.

Julie   Ah, right, terrific! What's that meant to be, more of you weaving a spell?! Richard may find that charming, but I don't.

Richard *enters.*

Richard   What do I find charming?

Julie   The suspense Miss Lambert tries to create with her stories.

Richard   Well that of course is true. And Mr Minken does it as well – even with the washing up! Just now everything had to be put away in exactly the right place to the absolute centimetre. (*Staring at the sacks of shredded paper.*) Even when he's getting rid of most of his collection. (*Quiet.*) I wonder

what causes somebody to be so obsessive they store their
whole professional life . . .?

(*He looks up.*) You realise at the very moment it is being
shown to the outside world it is being destroyed – which
makes it quite a privilege to be here.

Julie   That's one way of putting it.

Lambert   I'm glad you think so Richard.

Richard   But of course I've also realised you've been
cheating.

Lambert (*surprised*)   Cheating? In what way?

Richard   You've had all these reminders of the kids to look
at, a crib sheet of the past, no wonder you can remember so
many of them.

Minken *and* **Summers** *enter with a tray of coffee.*

Minken   Here – I hope – is the best coffee in London. A big
claim I know.

Lambert   But it's true.

Summers   Do you want milk? We all take it black.

Julie   Why doesn't that surprise me! Of course you do, you
never want to sleep again do you, any of you!

Lambert (*smiles*)   That may be right. (*Taking a cup.*) I hope it
is as strong as it usually is Frederick.

Minken   You both take milk do you?

Richard   I think we do, yes.

Julie   Yes, 'fraid so.

Richard (*grins*)   If that's alright, if that's allowed.

Minken (*pouring coffee*)   That is allowed yes.

Richard (*amused by his precision*)   Right . . . (*Staring down at one of the sacks for a moment.*) I can't help wondering if there is any of us here? Anything *we* ever did?

Julie   Yeah. Is there something of ours in this flat? I bet there's something . . .!

Minken   I've been waiting for that question.

Lambert   We thought you'd never ask.

Julie   Well I've been longing to ask – but something stopped me. So you've got something have you?

Lambert   Why of course.

Summers   He's very keen to show you I think.

Minken   Right . . . (*He moves to one of the filing cabinets and takes something out.*) Geraldine, if you could go to that one, (*indicating the other cabinet*) and take out a box labelled 14B, I think it's in the second draw down . . . right near the back . . .

Summers (*following his instructions*)   Yes, 14B, here it is.

Julie   Very impressive.

Minken   Meanwhile I have to get this working . . .

He indicates a black box in the corner that contains a slide projector. He begins to manoeuvre it into position.

Richard   So you have pictures of us do you?

Julie   Dressed as tubes of toothpaste no doubt or daffodils!

Lambert   I remember you two in assembly, your presentations. You were always together, and it was always a surprise.

Richard   At first I couldn't go up there at all, (*to* **Lambert**) but I remember you presenting my idea about Queen Victoria's elephants. It was amazing, my vision coming out of you! That was a great moment! After that I was able to go up there . . .

Julie (*watching the preparations apprehensively*)   What have you got Mr Minken? I'm a bit worried about what's going to come out of there!

Richard   *Waiting* to do it . . . I can remember that feeling so clearly. I was always really nervous.

Julie   Yes, frightened we'd stumble or it would get jumbled up.

Richard   Or nothing would come out at all.

The lights lower. A still image splashes on the back wall of the two children, aged 9½, standing side by side.

Minken   They are just still images I'm afraid, and in black and white because I prefer black and white.

Julie (*staring up at their younger selves*)   There we are, oh my God, there we are!

Richard   We look great I think.

Minken   And here's the soundtrack that goes with it.

Their younger voices come out of the speaker as the still mute image stares at us from the back wall. During their assembly **Minken** *changes the slides of them twice, each closer than the one before.*

Young Richard   This is our assembly, we are here to tell you about the kingdom . . .

Young Julie   The kingdom we are making, although it hasn't got a name yet.

Young Richard   All sorts of things will be forbidden there . . . and all sorts of *other* things will be allowed.

Julie   I don't remember doing this one, I really don't.

Richard   I do! Once I was on stage and the waiting was over I loved doing it . . .

Young Julie   Our kingdom will have the following rules.

Young Richard (*solemnly*)   There will be no practical jokes, no loud noises, no roller skating.

Richard   Quite right. All top priorities!

Young Julie   No exams and no wasps. There will be cars that clean themselves and you will be able to eat doughnuts at the dentist.

Young Richard   There will be no alarm clocks, burglar alarms or watches that squeak. And each morning at school there will be a special dream time . . .

Young Julie   When you can think whatever you like!

Young Richard   And during this special time you will be able to dream of what you are going to become.

The soundtrack breaks into a loud hiss; the image is still there but **Minken** *cuts the sound.*

Minken   That is all that survives.

Richard   What a list! I think I still agree with absolutely everything on it.

Julie   Not doughnuts at the dentist. I don't want my kids to be doing that.

Richard   I love our younger selves – when at last we got like that and could string a sentence together.

Lambert   Yes, the confidence coming off both of you.

Summers   Very poised.

Lambert   When I think of the two children that came to me for special help, who couldn't even read a single word, couldn't even decode signs on the street. And then look at you up there!

Richard   You gave us that confidence, undoubtedly.

Lambert   Well I started you on a journey anyway. (*She looks straight at him.*) One that led in your case Richard all the way to Number 10 Downing Street.

Momentary pause.

Richard   That's right.

Minken   You must tell us more about that Richard, about you addressing the Prime Minister.

Summers   We're very eager to hear about that.

Richard   Sure . . . sure. Why not? Anytime . . .

Minken   Give us a little more right now. (*Beadily.*) Go on!

Summers (*sharp*)   If you can.

Julie (*suddenly loud*)   He's already told you. He doesn't need to do anymore.

Richard   No, no Julie . . . this is alright.

Julie   It's not alright.

Pause.

Richard (*to the teachers*)   Of course I realise you know I was lying.

Lambert (*innocently*)   Were you Richard?

Richard   It was hardly difficult to spot. I was expecting to be caught out much earlier. (*He moves.*) I chose something I didn't think you'd know about . . .

Lambert   So what's the truth Richard?

Richard   Ah the truth . . . (*Stops.*) I've just got to think about the best way of doing this . . .

Julie   You don't have to tell them anything Richard.

Summers (*sitting very still*)   But he wants to.

Julie (*turning angrily on her*)   How on earth do you know that?

Summers   You knew he was lying of course . . .

Lambert   Just give us a little of the truth Richard.

Richard (*turns*)   Right just a little . . . let's try it this way. I did not work at Number 10 . . .

Slight pause.

But I *was* a security guard at the Home Office . . . with its shiny passages. How weird people looked coming towards me down that long white passage.

Minken (*beadily*)   They made you a security guard Richard?

Richard   Yes, funny isn't it – with my inability to concentrate for any length of time! And sure enough I began to fidget almost immediately . . .

Lambert   You wandered off didn't you Richard?

Richard   Yes indeed I did. I went for perambulations every now and then, till they got more frequent and bigger and bigger, until even the Home Office had to notice! And I got sacked of course. A security guard that w . . . w . . . wanders. (*He stammers for a moment.*) It's not ideal is it . . .

Julie   You don't have to do this Richard! Please don't. (*Suddenly.*) Why are you making him do this?

Lambert   Are we making him?

Julie   Yes –

Richard   And I have perambulated in other places . . . been a security guard in a warehouse full of microwave ovens . . . it was very easy to wander off there, with just the ovens watching! And I have been a messenger for various places or on reception –

Lambert   But you didn't always deliver the messages did you?

Richard That's right . . . sometimes I didn't. I've bobbled all my life . . . from one place to another . . . and of course I've bobbled away from my wife . . . my . . . my . . . my ex-wife and my son . . . (*his voice almost breaking*) my son who I don't see as often as I would like . . . (*He swallows.*) Both are gone.

Summers You don't see either of them?

Richard When I met Miss Lambert by the river, I was in the middle of trying to negotiate a time to see my son . . . he doesn't always want to see me . . .

Julie Stop there Richard . . . don't do anymore.

Richard No, no, just need to do one other thought. And that is . . . there have been moments, naturally, when the perambulations stopped and I've been in one place, and rather down, forced to be still . . . where the darkness sets in and you feel you're not going to get out of it for quite a while . . .

He stops.

Lambert Yes?

Minken And what happened Richard?

Richard Well it varied, but once or twice I've crawled across the kitchen floor on all fours . . . t . . . t . . . the smell of the floor really stays with you, the coins dropped down there and never picked up . . . or an earring from an old girlfriend by the fridge door . . . seeing one's life from that angle can be interesting, an angle one didn't expect. So . . . yes . . . you have got me . . . .you . . . g . . . g . . . g . . . got me completely, found me out.

(*He stands with his back to them.*) That couldn't be clearer.

Silence. He stands frozen for a moment, his back to them.

Julie (*softly*) Richard . . . are you alright?

Lambert We really didn't mean to upset you.

Julie   Didn't you?!

Summers   Why would we want to do that?

Julie   You tell me?! Richard is one of the brightest men I've ever met, why would you want to humiliate him?

Richard   No, no, this is fine. I think . . .

He looks round at them.

No, no, you did catch me out, but that's my fault. If I had left out Number 10 I would have probably got away with it . . . but I wanted to give you a conventional success story.

He looks up at the image on the back wall.

You shone my younger self at me and made me confess . . . And that was clever.

Summers   *You* asked to see it.

Richard   That's true. And I'm glad I did! (*He faces them.*) As it happens I did meet some of the most powerful people in the country really close, almost nose to nose – just as I said, but it was from checking their security passes, I was a man in a uniform. That's quite a good story, don't you think Miss Lambert?

Lambert   You mean the security guard who couldn't keep still?

Richard   That's right, the security guard that always wanders off.

Lambert   Yes, that is a story.

Minken   And now? What job are you doing now?

Richard   I'm in between jobs . . . but there are one or two possibilities . . . the other thing I was doing when I met Miss Lambert was gate-crashing a party on the lookout for a job – so we'll see where that leads . . .

Summers   You think that will lead somewhere?

Richard   It could. You know to be brutally honest, (*he smiles*) I would prefer to be what I am – whatever that might be – than a professional pollster any day.

Minken   And what are you Richard?

Richard   What am I? (*He moves.*) Sometimes I'm good on other people, but I'm never so good about myself. (*He turns.*) Well Mr Minken, I think I'm someone who is reasonably bright but who's brain went into those riffs of its own . . . and somehow I had to get control of that, and I'm fairly sure I have . . . (*He glances up at the image of his younger self.*) And this will surprise you, but I can look at him up there, I can look him in the eye, and feel OK. Feel no shame at all about what's happened, how things have turned out. (*He smiles.*) The best is yet to come.

Julie   Quite right Richard.

Richard   I intend to do something special at some stage in my life.

Minken *switches off the projected image.*

Julie   And my life you might be interested to know, is exactly as I said. I do work at the local health practice, I do have a partner . . . and we *are* in love! We are trying to have a baby! It is all real.

Summers   Did I hear any of us imply it wasn't?

Julie (*suddenly her anger boiling over*)   To hell with you, all three of you! You invite Richard for a meal and then do this! You had this planned I expect.

Richard   Don't worry about me Julie.

Lambert   What did we plan?

Julie   This is what it has come to has it, what you're really up to?! Cruising the streets looking for kids you used to teach, so you can coax them home and then beat them up about what has happened to them?!

Lambert   That's not what we do Julie.

Julie   Can't get your hands on the kids you really want, like those guys that were singing, so we'll do instead isn't that right?!

Minken   You two are not instead of anybody. Quite the reverse.

Julie (*furious*)   You should take a good look at what's happened to you for Christ sake!

Minken   Which is what?

Julie   Which is what?! Where shall I begin? I don't think you have the slightest idea how weird you've become –

Summers   Don't be so sure.

Julie   So thank you for the coffee, but we're going to get out of here now, aren't we Richard!

Richard   No. (**Julie** *looks at him sharply.*) This is good. This is useful.

Julie   Useful? In what way?

Richard   Now they know everything, it gives me licence. It allows me to ask whatever I want – especially of Miss Lambert . . .

Lambert   Is that what it does?

Richard   I think so, yes, because it makes us kind of equal.

Summers (*suddenly*)   Let me tell you Julie Shannon, no other child – or ex-pupil I should say – has ever been here before, isn't that right Mr Minken?

Minken   That is absolutely correct.

Julie (*very sharp*)   How fortunate we are!

Summers   So there's no question of us coaxing anybody here, and then thrashing things out of them – although I can think of a few examples where that would have been tempting.

Julie   What's the matter with you Miss Summers?

Summers (*innocently*)   With me?

Julie   Yes, you really are by far the worst you know.

Minken   That is not true.

Summers   You want to know what's the matter with me, I think that's simple. The children are the matter with me.

Richard   The children?

Summers (*calmly, coldly*)   Yes, they became the problem, though not when they were with us, when they left . . . gradually it happened.

I felt such excitement when I was younger, especially at the time of the sunflowers, when the Cold War was over! I couldn't wait to get into school.

Minken   She used to run to work.

Summers   Yes, what a future I thought they'd have, the children, everything was possible! They were the luckiest generation ever I thought – didn't need to worry about being obliterated at the press of a button, that huge weight was lifted. But what did they turn into when they left us? And I don't just mean the occasional armed robber, no, I mean those that got great jobs during the boom times. They had the best chance for their voices to be heard ever and what do they have to say? Where was anything original, anything that mattered?

And they expected so much for doing so little, I think that's what I minded most, you have no idea how high their expectations were – 'Give me fame now . . . give it to me! I don't need to do much surely, but give it to me. I have to have it now!'

Julie   I never thought that. And my kids won't think that.

Summers   It even started happening to our children before they left us, and we were powerless to stop it. The pictures they did for instance, that had been so surprising and fresh, suddenly became predictable, more 'grown up' in a horrible way. By the time they were seven they were so old already, their heads full of things you couldn't get past. I could really see what was taking them over, and it was frightening.

Julie   Right, now I understand – first you have a great time telling us stories about the city, trying to prove what a nightmare it is out there – and now you slag off all the kids you once taught!

Summers   I fell out of love with them certainly.

Julie   I can't imagine you loving anything Miss Summers.

Summers   I loved teaching. I loved it.

Lambert   Maybe more than any of us.

Summers   None of us wanted to go on after Elizabeth left, it was like winter descended on the school. It was easy to give up then. But since you asked what was the *matter* with me, I think I'm right in saying it was the children – is the children – which makes me so . . .

Julie   Bitter?

Summers   So unquiet.

Minken   They managed to lose their childhood.

Julie   I don't agree that's happened.

Minken (*switching the main lights on with a sharp flick*)   I have to get on, I have a schedule to keep to and I'm behind. (*He opens the cupboard and pulls out two heavy rubbish bags already tied up.*) *Everything* has to be out of here in a few days –

Richard   Can we help you?

Minken   Yes, in a moment you can. (*Indicating all the sacks.*) I need to get these outside for the dustmen, they hardly ever come and tomorrow is the day.

Lambert Except it's tomorrow already of course.

Julie Yes, we can help you with those, that's not difficult. I don't want to leave any of you angry that's for sure, it might not be wise. You might come after us!

Minken (*pulling the heavy sack*)   If I miss them it just all piles up outside, in a very unruly way –

Lambert Frederick's nightmare, anything being unruly.

Julie (*to* **Minken**)   Can we at least keep ourselves, stop our younger selves going into the shredder?

Richard Which is a pretty horrible end after all.

Minken The slides, I think I can possibly give you the slides. But don't ask me for anything else, please, *because it's going to go*!

Richard But you are still keeping some of it aren't you?! Like the toys, you've got to keep *those*?! You must!

Minken I have to be ruthless, (*gathering up the slides and tape*) so I can move on. (*Moving.*) Most of this has no meaning for me anymore anyway . . . (*Dangerous smile.*) So there you are, (*handing* **Richard** *and* **Julie** *the tape and slides*) and that is all you're getting.

Julie Thank you.

Richard (*to* **Lambert**)   And what are you keeping? Shouldn't you choose something from here before it all disappears?

Lambert No, I never keep anything from the past.

Richard Really, nothing?

Lambert Apart from the odd bit of furniture and the black and white TV, no.

Richard Why?

Lambert Because it's gone, that's why, it's over.

Summers (*moving to cupboard*)   I'm going to take a picture, one of the children's pictures if that's allowed. I'll just pick one at random, it's the only way. (*She plucks a picture from cupboard, takes a quick glance at it.*) Yes, this one will do . . . as a record. I'm different to you Elizabeth, I want something to remember those days by. (*She moves.*) And now I'm off into the night, what's left of it. (*Looking at* **Julie** *and* **Richard**.) Since they don't want me here.

Lambert (*urgent*)   Geraldine don't go . . .

Summers   No I'm not wanted, so I've gone.

Summers *exits.*

Julie (*staring after her*)   I've driven her away.

Lambert (*startled*)   I wasn't expecting her to go.

Richard   What do you need her for?

Lambert   Need her . . . of course I don't need her. (*Looking round for her bag.*) Anyway I have to make a move, I have to go too, I've got another stop before morning.

Richard   And where is that?

Lambert   I'm not telling you.

Richard   You're not telling me? Why not?

Lambert   There is nothing secret about it, it's just you can't come.

Richard   I want to come. I have to see what happens to you before morning Miss Lambert.

Lambert (*very sharp*)   What do you mean what happens to me?!

Richard *between her and the exit.*

Lambert   Richard just get out my way can you!

There is the sound of a tube train coming towards us.

Minken   There is another train . . . the second one they
run to deal with the rats and pigeons . . . that means it's later
than I thought. I've got to get these outside now. (*He begins to
move the sacks.*) Still so much to do!

Blackout.

*The sound of the tube train coming straight at us elides into the
sound of the steam train, a piercing whistle, and then the sound
of children's voices on a platform, heightened, agitated and adult
voices calling to them.*

FOURTH ASSEMBLY

*The sound of the steam trains die away as the agitated cries of the
children become more natural, busy chatter, as if they are sitting
cross-legged on a floor, waiting for assembly.* **Lambert** *and* **Minken**
*enter both in long black coats. He is holding a battered child's
suitcase, in dark-brown leather; it looks ancient and well travelled.
The children fall quiet. Both* **Lambert** *and* **Minken** *are more
youthful in their manner.* **Minken** *appears open and optimistic,
fired by a desire to communicate.*

Lambert *steps forward.*

Lambert   Today you are going to hear something that I'm
fairly sure you will never have heard before . . .

She looks out at us.

Something your parents – some of your parents – may be
surprised I let you hear . . . But I am going to . . .

She sits upstage, a still authoritative figure, watching. **Minken** *steps
forward.*

Minken   Children, you are right, Mr Minken doesn't
normally lead assembly, but today I'm going to show you
how I might not be here at all, what a very close-run thing
it was that I exist. I'm alive because of a meeting my father
had with a teacher. She was a woman he found loathsome, a

teacher he hated more than anybody else. And that meeting changed his life.

One day, in many years time, you might meet an ex-teacher of yours – it might even be me – and who knows what will happen?!

The sound of a female voice singing a lullaby in German.

My father was Austrian, he lived with his parents in Vienna before the Second World War. He had just had his tenth birthday and was feeling rather good about his life. He was a happy boy, one of his birthday presents had been this.

He produces with a flourish the toy flying boat out of one of his deep pockets.

A beautiful toy flying boat, he played with it all around the house and in the street, it was always in his pocket.

We hear the sound of an old school bell.

At school he had a very stern teacher, for he was in Frau Karlinger's class. Frau Karlinger was terribly strict but she also trusted her pupils absolutely. When each test was over, you marked your own paper in pencil as she called out the answers. And then she would ask, 'How many did you get right Emmanuel Minken?' 'Eight out of ten Frau Karlinger.' NOBODY EVER CHEATED. (*He stares at us.*) Amazing to think that isn't it!!

But then one day, not long after his birthday, my father lied because he had only got six out of ten. He *did* cheat! And somehow Frau Karlinger knew immediately. 'Eight out of ten you say, bring your paper up here Emmanuel Minken!'

And my father is shown to be a liar and a cheat in front of the whole class.

The sound of military vehicles rumbling close by and the sound of crowds cheering.

The very next day my father wakes up and the Nazis had walked into Vienna. If you were Jewish, and my father

and grandparents were Jewish, you were in great danger
of being arrested, beaten, or even worse. Things changed
totally in just a few hours. But my father didn't understand
any of this because it all happened quickly, and everything so
far in his life had been so good. Anything bad had been kept
from him.

So for a Jewish family it was a very good idea to try and get
out of Vienna that very day. Catch one of the last trains that
were being allowed to leave. But you have to run!

My grandfather, who never did anything in a hurry, said,
'We must take a very short holiday' – and they went to the
station with a few belongings.

We hear the sound of steam trains and piercing whistles.

My father has his flying boat with him and he is holding it
tight. Suddenly as they were about to get on a train a voice
calls out –

Summers *is standing upstage in a dark coat and hat.*

Summers (*as Karlinger calling across*)   Emmanuel Minken, is
that you?

Minken   My father is horrified to see Frau Karlinger
coming towards them

Summers   Emmanuel Minken, how fortunate to see you
here. I need to have a word with your parents.

Minken   My father knows she is going to expose him
as a cheat and liar – something his parents would never
forgive. He prays, 'God strike Frau Karlinger down, or at
the very least make her go away . . . God please don't let
this be happening!' And then Frau Karlinger says to my
grandfather –

Summers   Herr Minken, can I be of any help?

Piercing whistles sound all around us.

Minken   Help? How could she possibly be of any help? My father sees the station is full of police and Nazis searching the trains, pulling some people out of the carriages. But he is thinking they are just looking for criminals, there is nothing to stop *us* getting on the train!

And then my grandfather says an appalling thing – 'Frau Karlinger how very kind, maybe you can look after Emmanuel just for this afternoon . . .'

And my father starts crying out, 'No, let me stay with you, let me get on the train with you!'

All around the sound of the station in chaos.

Minken   'You will stay with Frau Karlinger all afternoon, there is no argument!' says my grandfather. And then he says 'I must make a list of a few things for you to do Emmanuel, just in case we are late back.'

And he starts writing a list, and he is *so slow*, his fountain pen doesn't seem to have enough ink, he keeps stopping and shaking it. And my father is thinking, 'He is taking so long, she is just bound to tell him now how I cheated!'

And still his father makes the list.

Summers (*urgent*)   Herr Minken, you can give that to Emmanuel later, let me take him now, and you can send him the list of things to remember. We must go now!

Minken   And my grandfather presses the unfinished list into my father's hand and with that Frau Karlinger starts pulling my father away, moving him very quickly out of the station, and when he looks back, his last sight of his parents, he sees his father standing there looking down at the fountain pen and shaking it, as all around him the station is in turmoil.

'Let me go' my father shouts, 'please, you must let me go!'

The sounds of the station dying away; we hear the sounds of bicycles and trams.

Summers   We will just have one cup of coffee, and wait a little till things are calmer. I think that's what we should do. We will spend the afternoon in a cafe together Emmanuel, and you can have a piece of cake.

The cafe tables start to appear around them, and tablecloths are spread, as church bells ring out.

Minken   And so while the Nazis rampage through the city they find a cafe down a side street. They stay there and have a cup of coffee and a piece of cake.

Summers *sits at a table in her dark coat,* **Minken** *stands hesitantly on the edge of the tables.*

Minken   And my father is thinking, 'What cruel joke is this, that I end up with my most frightening teacher, and have to spend a *whole* afternoon with her, how can this have happened?!'

Pause.

Of course the Nazis took my grandparents away to a camp and murdered them. And Frau Karlinger managed to get my father out of Austria to England through some English friends she had.

So Frau Karlinger saved my father from being killed. All his life hardly a day went by when he didn't wonder why she had been at the station in the first place. He never asked her. After the war he couldn't find her again . . . it can be difficult to find an ex-teacher.

Summers *disappears into the shadows.*

Minken   It must have been a complete accident mustn't it, that she was there at the station?

He takes out of his pocket a silver cigarette box, and out of the box he takes a piece of paper.

And this here is the unfinished list, the actual piece of paper handed to my father at the station. He kept it all his life.

It says 'First, always try to do your best, and always serve others as well as yourself . . .

Second, when you are doing your homework if you have to cross out too much, it is best to start all over again, however much you don't want to.'

And that is all there is, except the words 'Goodbye for now'.

He looks at the paper and then up at us.

I think that is why I like to collect things, that's what Mr Minken is famous for isn't it. Things from the past that bring everything back in an instant.

Because it is good to have a record.

Blackout

Scene Three

The sounds of the station surrounds us. And then some bland pop music breaks through the noises of the past.

The **Waitress** *throws a check tablecloth over the last table in the cafe. Five tables covered in red and white tablecloths, plastic ketchup containers, black wooden cafe chairs. A strip of fluorescent light, yellow and white along the back wall. The vent in the back wall shows light through it, the deep blue light just before dawn. The* **Waitress** *is not in uniform, she is wearing her own clothes, the atmosphere suggestive of a greasy spoon.* **Lambert** *enters the cafe and stands in her elegant coat as the music plays. She watches the* **Waitress** *spread the last tablecloth. The* **Waitress** *looks up.*

Waitress   Oh it's you. You're quite late today.

Lambert   Yes, a little later than usual. Mr Minken is here, and I have some guests.

Minken (*entering*)   Yes we're right behind.

Minken, Richard *and* **Julie** *enter.* **Minken** *is carrying a large carrier bag and a small suitcase.* **Richard** *is heaving a large suitcase.*

Richard   This is rather heavier than I thought.

Lambert   They insisted on keeping us company.

Minken   They did, but they are obligingly helping with my luggage. (*To* **Waitress**.) I'm transporting my belongings to a secure place, everything I have decided to keep is going into a lock-up I've got, not far from here –

Julie (*indicating* **Richard**)   I'm only here as his bodyguard, keeping him out of trouble.

Richard *places the suitcase near a table and turns.*

Richard   So it *is* open? From outside one couldn't be sure.

Waitress   Oh we don't close. There're not many twenty-four-hour cafes in the city, not in this area certainly, but we're open all through the night, every night of the week.

Lambert   And Nicky is here most nights.

Waitress   I am. It is usually busy till around 3.30. (*To* **Lambert**.) That's when I normally see you.

Julie (*to* **Lambert**)   So this is the 3.30 stop off!

Waitress   And then there is a lull till about 5.30 when the next wave hits, mostly truck drivers of course.

Lambert   We'll be out before then.

Waitress   Yeah, usually before they arrive I get some moments on my own, when I play music really loud, dance around here a bit, go a little mad. (*She smiles.*) Can do anything if I like, nobody watching!

Richard   But now *we're* all here.

Waitress   I guess I can cope.

Minken (*moving the large suitcase a few feet*)   Excuse me, this is my usual place, so we just need to move this, because this is where I sit when I'm here with Miss Lambert – and I have two eggs, bacon and six slices of white toast. (*The* **Waitress**

about to write this down.) But today I will just have some coffee and three slices of white toast.

Lambert   And just a tea for me, because we don't have long.

Julie   And a tea for me too please.

Richard   And I will have absolutely nothing, if that's alright.

Waitress (*slight smile*)   I think I can allow that yes. So two teas and a coffee, I'll get those.

Minken   And three slices of fresh white toast, it should still be warm.

Waitress   Of course.

Minken   And the music off please.

The **Waitress** *exits.* **Lambert** *is sitting at a downstage table, apart from the others.*

Richard   There she goes, the lone waitress. We've stopped her dancing around the deserted cafe. And you have your usual place Mr Minken.

The music stops.

Minken   Yes, about once a week I join Miss Lambert here after her walk. And we are slave to our routine aren't we, we eat a very early breakfast before the vile rush hour begins . . . but today we've got our timing wrong, I'm just a little bit earlier than normal –

Richard (*lightly*)   Yes, well I'm eager to see what you two get up to first thing in the morning, as the light comes up!

Lambert (*she smiles*)   I'm fairly certain I'm not a vampire Richard.

I think I can deal with a little sunlight.

Richard   Good. (*Sharp smile.*) It'll be a shock to see you like that.

Minken *has been looking inside his large carrier bag.*

He gets up sharply.

Minken   Excuse me . . . excuse me, I'm sorry I just need to check something, and I need to check it now.

He suddenly lifts the large suitcase onto one of the tables.

Julie   What's the matter? Have you forgotten something?

Minken   No, no, I just need to check the whereabouts of a certain item. (*Opens the suitcase.*) It could be in one of the pockets here.

Minken *moves some large dark books out of the suitcase.*

Lambert   His latest selection of what to keep.

Richard   So it's books, that's why it was so heavy.

Minken   Mostly books, yes. It's difficult to throw away books isn't it.

Lambert   Mr Minken has some very rare books.

Minken   Yes, but it's not one of those that I'm looking for . . . (*He looks in the pocket of the case.*) It's not in here.

Julie   Is it the slides? Is that what you're looking for?

Minken   No, I've got all the slides I want to keep. (*His manner is getting more agitated.*) I'll just try the other suitcase, but I know that is all books.

He opens the second smaller suitcase.

Richard   Can we help in some way? What have you lost?

Minken   No, no, I'm just looking for this particular thing, I need to find it . . . (*He stares into the smaller suitcase, then pulls out books.*) And it's not here . . . I can see it's not here!

Julie   You sure it's not in there, what is it?

Minken (*moving to carrier bag*)   So it has to be in here . . . I must have missed it the first time . . . it's *got* to be in here.

(*His manner getting more frantic.*) The awful thing is I carried this bag myself, because I was certain I had put the valuable item in here, I made sure I was responsible for it . . .

Lambert   It will be somewhere Frederick.

Minken   If this has happened, if I have lost it, I mean that is unthinkable. I put all this energy into clearing things out, I have destroyed my collection because I had to, but if I can't find one of the few things I regard as really precious . . .

Julie   What is it Mr Minken? We can't help you find it if we don't know what it is!

Minken (*pulling everything out of the bag*)   No, no there is absolutely no need for you to get involved . . . I know you don't want to leave me angry Julie, but there is –

Julie   Don't be stupid, I was the one who made you bring everything in from the car, because I'm only staying a moment. (*Sharp.*) So you have to tell me what it is?!

Minken (*looks up*)   It's a little box.

Richard   What kind of box?

Minken   Just a silver box.

Julie   What's in the box? It may have come open –

Minken   Just a toy, a stupid old toy and a list.

Richard   Like one of those old Dinky cars?

Minken   Yes, it's the flying boat, the one I showed you.

Lambert   I'm sure it's somewhere in there Frederick.

Minken   It's a piece of family history, I used to tell a story in assembly with it . . . you won't remember I know, my father and the toy flying boat.

Julie (*beginning to scour the floor*)   I remember a little I think, a station . . .

Richard   Yes, something to do with trains and not much time . . .?

Minken   Yes, it had something to do with trains . . . I can't expect you to remember everything.

Lambert   Some parents complained because he told that story, they said it was too upsetting . . .

Minken (*having completely emptied the carrier bag*)   Oh God, it's not here either.

Lambert   It won't be lost, you never lose anything.

Minken (*sinking back into his seat*)   I can't believe I have done this . . . I have lost the only thing I wanted. (*He covers his face with his hands.*) The one item above all others . . .

Julie   Come on Mr Minken, we can search for it, it's got to be somewhere.

Minken   The stupidity of it . . . it's the worst thing I've done . . . I can't bear it.

His face covered.

Julie   We'll go and look for it outside . . . it could have fallen out between here and the car.

Lambert   We'll all go and look.

Julie   No, I'll do it with Mr Minken. I'm usually good at finding things –

Richard   If anybody can find it, it's Julie.

Minken   It's gone, it was very small, we won't find it.

Julie (*very sharp*)   Mr Minken we have to try.

(**Minken** *doesn't respond.*) Something that means so much to you!

We'll retrace our steps, come on, the light will be coming up in a moment, it'll make it easier.

Minken (*standing slowly*)   I just don't understand why I
didn't put it in the suitcase . . . it was a mad thing to do.

Julie (*very firm*)   I'm going to look for it. Are you coming or
not Mr Minken?

Minken   I will come. (*He follows her out.*) I'm coming.

*They exit. The deep-blue light through the vent is just beginning to
brighten.*

Richard   She might find it, Julie's a bloodhound.

Lambert   I can believe that.

Richard   She'll scour every inch of pavement.

Lambert   Yes . . . (*Her tone changes, there is an edge to it.*) I
may not be able to stay to see if they find it though.

Richard   Going to leave me on my own guarding his
suitcases are you?

Lambert (*lightly*)   You can do that Richard I'm sure.

Richard   Why can't you stay?

Lambert   I just have things to do.

Richard   At 5am?

Lambert   At 5am, yes. Odd though it may seem, but I do.

Richard (*his tone suddenly very direct*)   Something happened
to you didn't it, that made you start these walks, there was a
day when everything seemed to change?

Lambert   No.

Richard   No?

Something obviously happened Miss Lambert.

Lambert   Absolutely not. Nothing *obvious* happened.
There was a particular forty-eight hours that perhaps had
something to do with me beginning this habit – and it is only
a habit – but it was nothing remarkable.

In the Underground one day –

Richard   Ah the Underground . . .

Lambert   Yes, down in the tube I saw a young couple arguing. The man takes the young woman by the hair, he holds her right over the edge of the platform, pointing her head straight at the rails and he is screaming at her – and nobody, not one of us on the platform, lifts a finger to help her. We just stood frozen, watching.

I had no idea why I didn't intervene.

She is not looking at him.

The next day I went to the zoo with my sister's grandchild. The Sumatran tiger was right up against the glass of his cage, it was the last Sunday of half-term, mothers were holding up their children, some fathers too, pressing them right up against the cage. The parents weren't speaking to each other but they were really competing – it was if they were crying out 'My child must get the best view of the tiger . . . no *my* child must, my child!' They were clustered against the glass pushing and elbowing each other for the best position, the tiger stares past them with contempt. The parents all squashed against the cage. 'My child must be first, my child!'

I felt this almost uncontrollable dislike of them, a horror of how unaware they were. (*Pause.*) And then the next day . . .

She stops.

Richard   Yes?

Lambert *looks up at him. At that moment the* **Waitress** *enters with the tray.*

Waitress   Your teas and coffee. I'm sorry it took a while, I wanted to make fresh coffee. (*She puts the tray down.*) The toast? Shall I leave it here for the gentleman?

Richard   Oh yes, thank you . . . He had to step out.

Waitress   If he is not back soon, I'll make some more.
(*Slight smile.*) I have the time! He did say he wanted warm
toast. He is always very particular about these things.

Richard   Thanks, if he needs some more we'll call you.

*The **Waitress** exits. The first signs of daylight increasing
imperceptibly.*

Richard   The next day Miss Lambert?

Lambert (*her tone dispassionate*)   I arrive at the school, it is
a normal morning assembly. (*The sound of children's voices
chattering, full of energy.*) I move onto the stage in front of
them, as I have done every day of term for twenty-five years.
(*The children fall silent.*) I look at them and I start shaking
. . . I feel it beginning, and I think I can stop this, but I
can't. I start to talk to the children, 'Today the story . . .'
(*She stops.*) 'The story today will be . . . the subject of today's
assembly will be . . .' (*She stares ahead.*) And nothing comes
out, no story. I can make no sound at all and my body, by
now my whole body is shaking. And I'm there in front of
the children, and they are completely silent, embarrassed,
shocked of course. Our eyes meet. I can't stop myself . . . I
leave the stage.

She pauses.

Something momentarily snapped. After all that time . . . it
was completely unexpected.

Her head is turned away. **Lambert**'s *voice is sharp and calm. But*
Richard *watches from a distance.*

Richard   It never happened again?

Lambert   It definitely did not, no. But I knew I couldn't do
the job much more.

Bit by bit I started a certain routine which continued after I
retired, a rhythm to my life which works, my only worry is
about occasionally losing track of time.

Richard (*very firm*)   No. You worry about what's going to happen next . . . (*He stares at her.*) Of what you're thinking of doing.

Lambert (*really sharp*)   I don't know what you can possibly mean by that Richard?!

Julie *and* **Minken** *enter.*

Julie   We've found it!

Minken   *She* found it yes.

Lambert   That's tremendous.

Richard   I knew she'd find it.

Minken   I thought we'd have no chance but there it was, on its side in the gutter. This little box.

Julie   And unopened. Nothing missing!

Minken (*opening the silver cigarette box*)   Just two small objects inside, a useless unfinished list and the flying boat . . . But it's a vital link –

Julie   To your family isn't it?

Minken   Yes, the only physical evidence left of my grandparents. (*Shutting box.*) How crazy it would have been if I had managed to get rid of this along with everything else!

Richard   But that didn't happen.

Minken   Just! By the skin of our teeth.

He begins to put the books back in the small suitcase.

Julie   I'm going to drive Mr Minken home now.

Minken   Yes, via the lock-up. All the energy I still have – and all I can use it for is moving things back and forth around London in suitcases.

He shuts the small suitcase. **Julie** *lifts it up.*

Julie   And really heavy cases at that –

Richard   Shall I?

Julie   No, we can manage, I've moved the car nearer . . .

Minken *is standing still, bent over his carrier bag.*

Lambert   What's the matter Frederick?

Minken   I was thinking why have I kept these books and got rid of almost everything else, my collection?! Was that wrong? I thought it was a way of moving on, but maybe I shouldn't have done it . . . (*He looks up.*) It's too late now.

Julie   It is too late now, yes.

Minken   Oh God yes, it's all gone.

Julie   But what a thing to do! How decisive – a new start. (*She puts her hands on his shoulders.*) Mr Minken, how very bold.

Minken   Bold? I don't know if I've ever been bold in what I've done, not really . . . but yes it was decisive. There's no way of bringing it back.

Julie   No . . .

Minken   Irreversible . . . I've done it. (*He goes to pick up the large suitcase.*) I have no idea what I'm going to do with my life now, what will happen next . . .

But I better get these things under lock and key before I leak anything else precious. (*Sharp smile.*) And then home, Julie's taking me home, she's looking after me!

Julie   Just for this morning.

Minken   Elizabeth, I'll call you tomorrow. (*He turns.*) Richard, I've absolutely no clue when I'll see you again.

Richard   I am sure we will though.

Minken   Maybe in another twenty years, and then I'll cook for you again!

But it won't be in this city, that's for sure!

Julie (*by exit*)   Look the sun is nearly up . . . we're going to be seeing in the dawn together Mr Minken.

Minken   Who would have thought . . .! What a strange turn of events that is!

They exit.

Lambert   The sun's almost up. She's right.

Richard   And that's a little unnerving isn't it.

Lambert   Why should it be unnerving? I just need to get on . . .

Richard   You don't want to stay because you don't want to face the morning.

Lambert   What?!

Richard   You heard me.

Lambert   That is absolutely not true Richard.

Richard   Isn't it? When was the last time you were outside in the morning?

Lambert   Don't be ridiculous. I'm often out and about first thing. When we met by the river it was daylight remember?

Richard   No, that was in the evening. I think you always get back just before morning breaks and don't go out until the day is starting to die.

Lambert   I have no idea why you think that, that's totally wrong –

Richard   Prove it to me.

Lambert   How?

Richard   Show me you don't have to run away.

Lambert   I have no intention of running away I assure you, but what you don't seem to be able to accept is that I have things to attend to, which I need to do.

She is gathering up her bag; the sounds of the city are starting.

Richard   Of course. (*Turns.*) Hear that?

We hear the distant rumble.

Lambert   Hear what?

Richard   You can just begin to hear the city waking . . . remember what you made us do in class? Always being aware of the rumble of the city . . . any moment it will get louder . . . the first planes coming in . . . but those sounds are alright aren't they Miss Lambert?

Lambert   What do you mean alright? Of course they're alright!

Richard   You can deal with those, but there's one sound you dread hearing isn't there in the morning – the one you least expected ever having to worry about.

The sound of kids going to school.

We hear, faintly at first, the sound of children's voices.

Lambert   Richard you can't just guess like that and hope to find something out.

Richard   Can't I? I don't think I'm guessing – when you stopped work you hated the start of the day didn't you, hearing them go down the street in the morning and then later the sound of the playground ringing out from a nearby school?

We hear the exuberant sound of the kids at play.

Lambert   Why on earth would that be true?

Richard   Not because you have fallen out of love with the kids like Miss Summers, but because you thought you'd failed, very powerfully you felt that. You'd had a school, you'd tried to touch so many imaginations, now the chance had gone for ever.

Lambert   That's nonsense. It is a great mistake to think you can ever know what somebody else is really feeling – especially somebody you hardly know.

Richard   Is it? I don't think so, not for me, and certainly not at this moment – the sense of loss you had started making everyday sounds unbearable didn't it? . . . (*Looking at her.*) Admit it.

Lambert   I will not admit that.

Richard   The sound of the morning, in a way it became terrifying.

Lambert   You really think I'm terrified of the morning?!

Richard   The nights were different though weren't they, that's what you discovered.

The sound of the night begins; first the tube tunnel.

You felt you could face the night, all that energy you still had –

Lambert   I do still have energy, Richard, yes!

Richard   So you turn the day on its head, only living at night – when you could just observe things without feeling you should be shaping them, influencing them . . .

Now we hear the boy, **Callum**'s *voice.*

And even meeting a psychopathic kid that killed his mother – somehow that's so much less alarming than the sound of normal children setting off in the morning. (*Looking at her.*) I'm *close* aren't I?

Lambert   You're not that close, no.

Richard   Oh I think I'm very close. The pain is not there at night, not to the same extent. And it soon becomes really addictive doesn't it, only going out and about then and slipping back before sunrise?!

Lambert   If it is an addiction it is an entirely harmless one.

Richard (*looking straight at her, his tone is firm*)   But in the back of your mind you're thinking all I'm actually doing is floating, I'm apart from everything really, and there'll come a moment – I don't know when you say to yourself but there'll come a moment – when it is right to bring things to an end.

Lambert   No! That is wrong, no –

Richard   And you even take a walk with that in mind up to Archway, not that far from your old school, up to that bridge where many people have finished things –

Lambert   I do not! I have never been there –

Richard   Where London is tilted at such an odd angle . . .

Lambert   I have never walked up there, never been there in my life! I warn you, you should not go on with this –

Richard   Then somewhere else, it happened somewhere else. *You had that moment, I am sure you did.* But you knew you weren't quite ready then.

The sunlight really hits the set.

Lambert   Richard, that is enough, you will not go any further, I forbid you to go further.

Richard   Do you?

The sunlight is increasing all the time. **Lambert** *is standing, her head turned away, unable to look at him.*

Richard   The light is up and you can't move.

Lambert (*fighting back tears, her head turned away*)   I can't move . . . no.

Richard (*staring at her hunched away from him*)   The opposite of a child that is afraid of the dark, a teacher that is afraid of the light.

It's like a story you never told us.

Lambert   I would never have told you *this story* . . .

Richard   Caught by the sunrise. (*He watches her.*) And you can't move Elizabeth . . .

Lambert   Are you trying to make me really cry this time? (*Her voice cracking.*) To make me weep in front of you? Is that what you're after? Because I will, if that's what you want. If that will make you stop.

She is fighting back tears; she cannot move.

Richard   Look at me and tell me I'm wrong and I'll stop. (*Momentary pause.*) Tell me I'm wrong.

Silence. **Lambert** *doesn't look at him.*

Lambert   You're not completely right.

Richard   I am about *this*. You walk some more nights, after what nearly happened, happened – waiting for that feeling of completeness, of what else is there? . . . to close around you and it's getting nearer all the time, really close . . .

Lambert (*now she looks at him*)   And?

Richard   And then you ran into me.

Lambert   I did run into you Richard, yes, by chance.

Richard   Or somehow you summoned me up!

Lambert   Oh how I wish I did have the power to do that with people . . .

Richard   We meet. And there I am, one of the originals you created – one of the many no doubt, whatever Miss Summers says. Julie and I, your originals, your successes.

Lambert (*suddenly sharp, powerful*)   An interesting view of success Richard! You're currently unemployed, you've been fired from several jobs, you've suffered from depression, you've left your family –

Richard   Oh you're not going to win that way Elizabeth, you can't possibly!

Lambert   No? What way is that?

Richard   You can't make me feel bad about myself, you did your job too well. Whenever I worried about being found out, I thought about what you'd taught me, that I *could* manage things after all. I defeated my depression.

And though there seems nothing to show for it – for some reason I have confidence, I told you, the best is yet to come. I'm absolutely clear about that.

Lambert   I'm glad you can read the future so easily. (*Suddenly moves.*) When you said all I've been doing is floating, since I've left the school – I don't know how you got so close with that.

Sometimes when I'm walking – walking on damp pavements – I feel I'm leaving no trace of any footsteps, it's like one's past has melted away, like it was never there in fact . . . and it doesn't count for anything at all. Everything I've dedicated my life to . . . just vanished. (*Pause. She is not looking at him.*) And then of course one begins to feel one's vanishing oneself. And that must happen . . .

Richard   Everything you've done is gone?

Lambert   Yes.

Richard   But yours is an extraordinary career Elizabeth!

Lambert   What?! I've merely been head of a school, there is nothing the least extraordinary about that –

Richard   In your case there was. And it's about to enter a new phase.

Lambert (*very sharp*)   A new phase? And what might that be?

Richard   Well I don't know for sure, do I . . .

Lambert   No. There's no way you can know that. And let's be very clear Richard, whatever you say, you can't make everything come right.

My life is what it is. You have to realise that.

Richard   I expect I realise that.

Lambert (*with real force*)   You find a woman lying in the open air, by a litter bin. Your first impression was right Richard! *It was how it seemed*. You are not going to change things.

Richard   No, of course not.

Pause.

But if I can borrow something else from you, just for a moment, I could try my first venture in time travel . . .

Lambert   To where Richard?

Richard   Well since it is a first attempt, maybe not very far, maybe just a few weeks.

Lambert   A few weeks? That certainly isn't ambitious, no.

Richard   That's right.

Lambert   And that would have no purpose at all, would it?!

Richard *is suddenly pulling back one of the tables to create a space. He starts putting a line of chairs in a row.*

Richard   Even though we're going into the future, rather than the past, we should do what you did . . .

So if we had some of Mr Minken's tapes with us now –

Lambert   You can't have tapes of the future.

Richard   No, but it's just a month ahead from now, we can guess . . . what would we hear?

Maybe it's the other end of the day, the usual sounds of the city, ringing with sirens, and car alarms, and a passing car radio . . . (*We hear the sounds pass us.*) And maybe we're by the river. On a bench.

The chairs are lined up; he looks across at her.

Come here.

Lambert   Come over there and lie on an imaginary bench, I don't think so.

Richard   No, no lying this time. Come and sit on an imaginary bench. (**Lambert** *hesitates.*) Just for a minute.

Lambert *moves over and sits next to him on the row of chairs, but a little apart. The white light imperceptibly begins to shift into evening.*

Lambert   I'm here . . .

Richard   Yes we're by the river, staring out. And you're still stalking the city, still coming across very particular things.

Lambert   Well that at least sounds correct.

Richard   And maybe Julie is with us . . .

Julie *enters wearing a different bright colour to earlier in the scene.*

Richard   She's in her usual bold colours, the slightly eccentric combinations she likes.

Julie *sits at the other end of chairs, again slightly apart.*

Richard   She's got a book with her, which she is reading.

Lambert   Julie reading a book?!

Richard   Yes. We don't know if she is pregnant or not. We don't know whether to ask her, so we don't. But we're fairly sure she'll give us a bulletin eventually in her usual way.

Julie (*looks up from her book*)   I'm not yet, not quite, fucking hell what a wait!

But I will be! It's close.

The face on the back wall, Titus Meredith, begins to appear again.

Richard   And maybe since we're by the river the bells from St Paul's are beginning to ring out, and because it is that time of the day, like any great city, just before the light goes, the view looks rather stunning and mysterious, if only for a moment . . . full of possibilities.

The bells ring in the distance.

And I will be as eager as always, to hear the scary things you've witnessed as you've moved around London. And you'll have some really good new examples . . .

Lambert   No doubt I will, yes . . .

Richard   You can tell us terrifying stories because I love to hear them. And the walks show no sign of decreasing . . .

Lambert   That is true too. They are absolutely not decreasing.

Pause.

Richard   But there is a difference.

Lambert (*sharp*)   Is there? And what is that.

Richard   The difference is that you are walking by day.

Watching what's happening in the city by daylight.

Lambert *gets up, moving away from the row of chairs.*

Lambert   By day?

Richard   Yes. You walk out of the house after breakfast.

You lose the fear of the morning.

The sound of children's excited voices moving round us.

You walk through the children going to school, they flow around you.

That is the difference Elizabeth.

Pause.

Lambert   That *is* a difference . . . I don't think so.

Richard   Oh yes, she makes herself walk by day. (*Powerful, straight at her.*) That is what she does.

Lambert *looks across at him.*

Richard (*quieter*)   And the sound of the kids . . . (*the children's voices rise and then stop suddenly*) have become no more disturbing than any other sound . . .

Lambert *keeps her distance.*

Richard   For example as we sit in that little garden, we hear someone biting into an apple really loud, the noise of teeth going into a fresh apple.

The loud sound of somebody biting into an apple.

Julie (*looking up from her book*)   What the fuck was that?!

Richard   Oh that's just the sound of a murdered actor.

He indicates Titus Meredith's face on the back wall.

(*To* **Lambert**.) We've got to hear it sooner or later haven't we, that was bound to happen, because whatever you told us, however strange the story . . . it was always true, wasn't it Elizabeth.

Lambert   Always.

Silence.

Richard   So?

Lambert   So?

Richard   My time travelling? What do you think?

Pause.

Lambert *looks up, meeting his gaze.*

Lambert   That's an interesting story Richard.

Richard   And so it's bound to come true.

Lambert (*softly, warm*)   We'll see.

Richard   It will. I think I know how to tell them by now. Stories.

He looks across at her.

I had a rather good teacher after all.

Fade.

Methuen Drama Student Editions

Methuen Drama Modern Plays

include work by

Edward Albee
Jean Anouilh
John Arden
Margaretta D'Arcy
Peter Barnes
Sebastian Barry
Brendan Behan
Dermot Bolger
Edward Bond
Bertolt Brecht
Howard Brenton
Anthony Burgess
Simon Burke
Jim Cartwright
Caryl Churchill
Complicite
Noël Coward
Lucinda Coxon
Sarah Daniels
Nick Darke
Nick Dear
Shelagh Delaney
David Edgar
David Eldridge
Dario Fo
Michael Frayn
John Godber
Paul Godfrey
David Greig
John Guare
Peter Handke
David Harrower
Jonathan Harvey
Iain Heggie
Declan Hughes
Terry Johnson
Sarah Kane
Charlotte Keatley
Barrie Keeffe

Howard Korder
Robert Lepage
Doug Lucie
Martin McDonagh
John McGrath
Terrence McNally
David Mamet
Patrick Marber
Arthur Miller
Mtwa, Ngema & Simon
Tom Murphy
Phyllis Nagy
Peter Nichols
Sean O'Brien
Joseph O'Connor
Joe Orton
Louise Page
Joe Penhall
Luigi Pirandello
Stephen Poliakoff
Franca Rame
Mark Ravenhill
Philip Ridley
Reginald Rose
Willy Russell
Jean-Paul Sartre
Sam Shepard
Wole Soyinka
Simon Stephens
Shelagh Stephenson
Peter Straughan
C. P. Taylor
Theatre Workshop
Sue Townsend
Judy Upton
Timberlake Wertenbaker
Roy Williams
Snoo Wilson
Victoria Wood

Methuen Drama Contemporary Dramatists
include

John Arden (two volumes)
Arden & D'Arcy
Peter Barnes (three volumes)
Sebastian Barry
Dermot Bolger
Edward Bond (eight volumes)
Howard Brenton
 (two volumes)
Richard Cameron
Jim Cartwright
Caryl Churchill (two volumes)
Sarah Daniels (two volumes)
Nick Darke
David Edgar (three volumes)
David Eldridge
Ben Elton
Dario Fo (two volumes)
Michael Frayn (three volumes)
David Greig
John Godber (four volumes)
Paul Godfrey
John Guare
Lee Hall (two volumes)
Peter Handke
Jonathan Harvey
 (two volumes)
Declan Hughes
Terry Johnson (three volumes)
Sarah Kane
Barrie Keeffe
Bernard-Marie Koltès
 (two volumes)
Franz Xaver Kroetz
David Lan
Bryony Lavery
Deborah Levy
Doug Lucie

David Mamet (four volumes)
Martin McDonagh
Duncan McLean
Anthony Minghella
 (two volumes)
Tom Murphy (six volumes)
Phyllis Nagy
Anthony Neilsen (two volumes)
Philip Osment
Gary Owen
Louise Page
Stewart Parker (two volumes)
Joe Penhall (two volumes)
Stephen Poliakoff
 (three volumes)
David Rabe (two volumes)
Mark Ravenhill (two volumes)
Christina Reid
Philip Ridley
Willy Russell
Eric-Emmanuel Schmitt
Ntozake Shange
Sam Shepard (two volumes)
Wole Soyinka (two volumes)
Simon Stephens (two volumes)
Shelagh Stephenson
David Storey (three volumes)
Sue Townsend
Judy Upton
Michel Vinaver
 (two volumes)
Arnold Wesker (two volumes)
Michael Wilcox
Roy Williams (three volumes)
Snoo Wilson (two volumes)
David Wood (two volumes)
Victoria Wood

Methuen Drama Modern Classics

Jean Anouilh *Antigone* • Brendan Behan *The Hostage* • Robert Bolt
A Man for All Seasons • Edward Bond *Saved* • Bertolt Brecht *The
Caucasian Chalk Circle* • *Fear and Misery in the Third Reich* • *The Good
Person of Szechwan* • *Life of Galileo* • *The Messingkauf Dialogues* •
Mother Courage and Her Children • *Mr Puntila and His Man Matti* •
The Resistible Rise of Arturo Ui • *Rise and Fall of the City of
Mahagonny* • *The Threepenny Opera* • Jim Cartwright *Road* • *Two &
Bed* • Caryl Churchill *Serious Money* • *Top Girls* • Noël Coward
Blithe Spirit • *Hay Fever* • *Present Laughter* • *Private Lives* • *The Vortex* •
Shelagh Delaney *A Taste of Honey* • Dario Fo *Accidental Death of an
Anarchist* • Michael Frayn *Copenhagen* • Lorraine Hansberry *A
Raisin in the Sun* • Jonathan Harvey *Beautiful Thing* • David Mamet
Glengarry Glen Ross • *Oleanna* • *Speed-the-Plow* • Patrick Marber
Closer • *Dealer's Choice* • Arthur Miller *Broken Glass* • Percy Mtwa,
Mbongeni Ngema, Barney Simon *Woza Albert!* • Joe Orton
Entertaining Mr Sloane • *Loot* • *What the Butler Saw* • Mark Ravenhill
Shopping and F***ing • Willy Russell *Blood Brothers* • *Educating Rita* •
Stags and Hens • *Our Day Out* • Jean-Paul Sartre *Crime Passionnel* •
Wole Soyinka • *Death and the King's Horseman* • Theatre Workshop
Oh, What a Lovely War • Frank Wedekind • *Spring Awakening* •
Timberlake Wertenbaker *Our Country's Good*

Methuen Drama World Classics

include

Jean Anouilh (two volumes)
Brendan Behan
Aphra Behn
Bertolt Brecht (eight volumes)
Büchner
Bulgakov
Calderón
Čapek
Anton Chekhov
Noël Coward (eight volumes)
Feydeau (two volumes)
Eduardo De Filippo
Max Frisch
John Galsworthy
Gogol
Gorky (two volumes)
Harley Granville Barker
  (two volumes)
Victor Hugo
Henrik Ibsen (six volumes)
Jarry

Lorca (three volumes)
Marivaux
Mustapha Matura
David Mercer (two volumes)
Arthur Miller (six volumes)
Molière
Musset
Peter Nichols (two volumes)
Joe Orton
A. W. Pinero
Luigi Pirandello
Terence Rattigan
  (two volumes)
W. Somerset Maugham
  (two volumes)
August Strindberg
  (three volumes)
J. M. Synge
Ramón del Valle-Inclán
Frank Wedekind
Oscar Wilde

For a complete catalogue
of Methuen Drama titles
write to:

Methuen Drama
Bloomsbury Publishing Plc
49–51 Bedford Square
London WC1B 3DP

or you can visit our website at:

www.methuendrama.com